US AIR FORCE/JOSHUA PLUEGER

Foreword

When compiling a magazine devoted to intelligence, surveillance, and reconnaissance two factors pertain: the vast array of systems used to conduct the role, and its complexity.

That systems employed for this critical element of modern planning range from small handheld drones weighing a few pounds, through four-engine RC-135 Rivet Joint aircraft with a max gross take-off weight of 297,000lb, to satellites in orbit around the earth.

Content selected for this edition includes a section explaining ISR and the types of intelligence used by Western militaries in both peacetime and during conflict. We then feature many of the most prolific types of manned and unmanned aircraft used by NATO and non-NATO nations. These include the RC-135 Rivet Joint (a derivative of the Boeing 707), U-2 Dragon Lady (Gary Powers' plane), the MQ-4 Triton (an unmanned long-endurance maritime surveillance platform), the venerable EP-3E Aries II and the RAF's Beechcraft King Air-based Shadow. Each section provides details of the aircraft and its sub-systems, and where possible operations.

Lastly, we've devoted a large section to commercially-owned aircraft used for ISR duty on behalf of Western militaries and government organisations.

Whatever your interest in aviation, *ISR - Spies in the Sky* is packed with highly-capable aircraft types used to feed governments and military commanders with the vital intelligence required to govern and conduct 21st century combat.

Mark Ayton
Editor

Contents

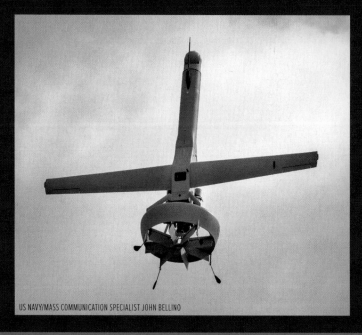

US NAVY/MASS COMMUNICATION SPECIALIST JOHN BELLINO

MATTHEW CLEMENTS

LUFTWAFFE

FÖRSVARSMAKTEN

ISBN: 978 1 80282 849 8

Editor: Mark Ayton
Senior editor, specials: Roger Mortimer
Email: roger.mortimer@keypublishing.com
Cover design: Steve Donovan
Design: SJmagic DESIGN SERVICES, India
Advertising Sales Manager: Brodie Baxter
Email: brodie.baxter@keypublishing.com
Tel: 01780 755131
Advertising Production: Becky Antoniades
Email: rebecca.antoniades@keypublishing.com

SUBSCRIPTION/MAIL ORDER
Key Publishing Ltd, PO Box 300, Stamford,
Lincs, PE9 1NA
Tel: 01780 480404
Subscriptions email: subs@keypublishing.com

Mail Order email: orders@keypublishing.com
Website: www.keypublishing.com/shop

PUBLISHING
Group CEO and Publisher: Adrian Cox

Published by
Key Publishing Ltd, PO Box 100, Stamford,
Lincs, PE9 1XQ
Tel: 01780 755131 **Website:** www.
keypublishing.com

PRINTING
Precision Colour Printing Ltd, Haldane,
Halesfield 1, Telford, Shropshire. TF7 4QQ

DISTRIBUTION
Seymour Distribution Ltd, 2 Poultry Avenue,
London, EC1A 9PU
Enquiries Line: 02074 294000.

KEY
Publishing

MAIN IMAGE • *The Ultra Long Endurance Aircraft Platform (Ultra LEAP) consists of a high-performance, cost-effective, sport-class commercial airframe converted to a fully automated system with autonomous take-off and landing capabilities. The Air Force Research Laboratory's Center for Rapid Innovation (CRI) successfully completed initial flight tests for the revolutionary Unmanned Aerial System (UAS) with a customisable suite of intelligence, surveillance and reconnaissance tools that supports extended missions.* COURTESY ARTWORK/AIR FORCE RESEARCH LABORATORY

Intelligence, Surveillance and Reconnaissance

ISR is a broad topic with an exhaustive number of terms, systems, and applications. We explain the fundamentals and feature some of the latest systems.

What does the slightly awkward military term 'intelligence, surveillance and reconnaissance' mean?

To most people, the meaning of the individual words is such: intelligence is the ability to acquire and apply knowledge and skills; surveillance refers to keeping watch over something, such as your home with a security camera; and reconnaissance means taking a peek at something of interest to you such as the location of a new house.

Among the militaries of the West, the term intelligence, surveillance, and reconnaissance (ISR) refers to a mission, one that encompasses acquiring information of military or political value (intelligence); keeping a close watch over someone or something (surveillance); and observing an area or region to locate enemy forces and equipment or to ascertain strategic infrastructure.

US Air Force doctrine states: "Intelligence operations illuminate the strategic, operational, and tactical environment, clarify adversary intentions, and are critical to commander decision-making across the competition continuum. Such operations encompass all-domain intelligence collection through the full spectrum of sensor capabilities and the integrated processing, exploitation, analysis, and production activities at the unit level, air operations centres, distributed ground stations, and national production centres."

Intelligence products are disseminated to tactical, operational, and strategic users.

US Air Force doctrine also states: "ISR is an activity that synchronises and integrates the planning and operation of sensors; assets; processing, exploitation, and dissemination (PED) systems; and analytic systems or capabilities. As a result, ISR is often the first capability a combatant commander requests before commencing operations. Moreover, ISR operations often persist after other operations have ceased. They are continuous, and in high demand.

"The goal for intelligence is to enable decision advantage by providing a comprehensive and cohesive awareness of the operating environment. Doing so requires an integrated approach; one that combines data and intelligence from joint, departmental, national, and multinational capabilities. Towards this aim, US Air Force intelligence forces integrate, fuse, tailor, and analyse collected information and data to deliver timely intelligence, when

LEFT • *A civilian contractor embarked with the 31st Marine Expeditionary Unit, prepares to take hold of a V-BAT drone once it lands aboard the amphibious dock landing ship USS Rushmore (LSD 47) in the Philippine Sea on August 24, 2022.*
US MARINE CORPS/LCPL MANUEL ALVARADO

and where needed, anywhere around the globe."

Intelligence operations are domain, sensor, and service agnostic (interoperable) and focused on meeting information requirements and providing actionable intelligence to commanders at the right time and place.

Intelligence vs ISR

The US Air Force doctrine document also explains the subtle differences between the two terms: Intelligence and ISR, which it says are often used interchangeably.

The air force defines intelligence in three ways. The product resulting from the collection, processing, integration, evaluation, analysis, and interpretation of available information concerning foreign nations, hostile or potentially hostile forces or elements, or areas of actual or potential operations. The activities that result in the product, and the organisations conducting such activities.

Similarly, the air force defines ISR in two ways. The integrated operations and intelligence activity that synchronises and integrates the planning and operation of sensors; assets; and processing, exploitation, and dissemination systems in direct support of current and future operations. The organisations or assets conducting such activities.

In discerning between the two terms, intelligence and ISR, the air force says: "It is important to identify their purpose or aim. ISR activities produce information and data. Through the joint intelligence process, information and data is then used to produce intelligence.

A key component of the intelligence process is the intelligence analyst, about which the air force says: "Intelligence analysts retain a theatre-wide perspective of threats, prioritise their work based on the commander's intent, and synchronise intelligence with plans and operations."

An analyst's work involves assessing and anticipating risk posed by threats, collaborating with other agencies to leverage analytical expertise, and exploit all sources of information and intelligence through fusion.

ISR Air Component

The US Air Force air component uses three integrated capabilities

Latest Equipment

Air Force Distributed Common Ground System

The Air Force Distributed Common Ground System (AF DCGS) is a weapon system used by a combat air force for planning, direction, collection, processing, exploitation, production, dissemination, and problem centric, sensor-agnostic analysis of data through a combination of reach back, forward support, and collaboration.

The system can connect, direct and exploit sensors and transform multi-source/multi-domain data into what is referred to as actionable intelligence which is used to find, fix, and target adversary forces and shorten the kill chain.

The AF DCGS system is scalable and capable of deployed and globally distributed operations.

The US Air Force DCGS is a key provider to and consumer of the sensing grid and the Advanced Battle Management System, the air force initiative for Joint All Domain Command and Control, the concept for connecting sensors from all the US armed services.

The term sensing grid comprises four elements: sensors, digital infrastructure, orchestration, and making sense of the data.

The mission of the AF DCGS is to provide Joint Task Force (JTF) commanders, air component commanders, unified commands, and other organisations with global, time-sensitive ISR across the spectrum of military operations.

Designated the GSQ-272 and called Sentinel, the AF DCGS is capable of exploiting intelligence data from manned platforms, remotely piloted aircraft, non-traditional ISR platforms, national and commercial satellites, and other collection systems.

AF DCGS serves as the main sense-making organisation within the US Air Force ISR sensing grid. It has access to a multitude of sensors and data across the intelligence community, as well as publicly available information.

Analysts employ Artificial Intelligence (AI), Machine Learning (ML), and Automation, Augmentation (AAA) technologies to search for multi-source/multi-domain intelligence across the tactical/national sensor grid and within federated databases. This enables sensor-agnostic analysis and exploitation to address joint operational requirements by providing a common means to provide intelligence to field commanders and the Air Operations Center mission requirements to support the kill chain across the full range of military operations.

Analysts use all available data and AAA to enhance their understanding of intelligence and targeting problem sets and provide the required intelligence.

Currently, AF DCGS comprises eight core sites, three remote sites, six SIGINT distributed mission sites, three Air National Guard full-motion video sites, three support sites, one training site, and three integration and test sites.

As a networked weapon system, all DCGS sites are linked which maximises its effectiveness and efficiency by leveraging workforce and intelligence resources and ensuring continuity of operations. Processing, exploitation, and dissemination (PED) tasks are routinely transferred from one core site to another without moving intelligence personnel.

The lead DCGS wing publishes a daily PED tasking order to task each site, in which airmen are organised around problem-sets and formed into mission management teams and analysis and exploitation teams.

The system currently supports ongoing operations from forward deployed and bases in the US and overseas.

Products supplied by the AF DCGS include fused geospatial intelligence (GEOINT), signals intelligence (SIGINT), and measurement and signature intelligence (MASINT), tailored to combat forces for all levels of conflict.

The AF DCGS is migrating to an open architecture to enable the rapid integration of new and/or improved sensor capabilities, and improved mission applications. The system operates in a hybrid cloud comprising a mix of private on-site and public commercial cloud architecture.

The AF DGCS program is managed in four efforts:

GEOINT and SIGINT transformation rapidly integrates new and updated capabilities that enable integration of new sensors, data types, sensor planning, and command and control capabilities into the open architecture framework.

Multi-INT transformation rapidly integrates new and updated enterprise applications to include voice and chat communications, collaboration and situational awareness, multi-INT fusion, and artificial intelligence, machine learning, and automation, augmentation data analysis capabilities.

Network infrastructure transformation continues to update the AF DCGS infrastructure to a cyber-resilient, open, scalable, commercial-based architecture, improves data ingest, transfer, and storage capabilities, and handles the integration of additional line-of-site capabilities.

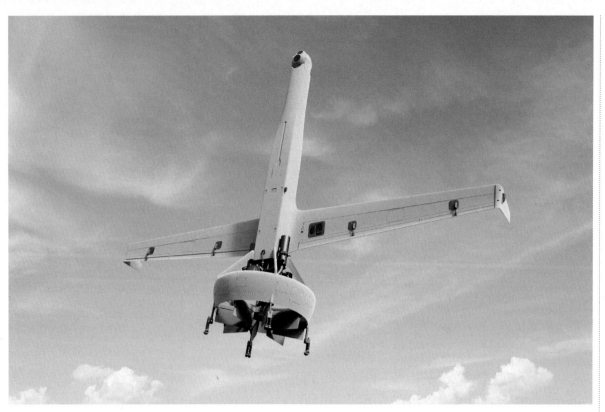

LEFT • *The Northrup Grumman and Shield AI V-BAT is one of five project agreement holders for the FTUAS INC 2 Rapid Prototyping effort.*

to support the acquisition of intelligence information, each provided by an Air Operations Centre.

1. Battlespace characterisation gives an understanding of an adversary by examining its capabilities, tactics, dispositions, centres of gravity, and courses of action within the operating environment. The air force deems battlespace characterisation as critical for providing indications and warnings, identifying potential vulnerabilities to forces, and identifying opportunities to achieve objectives. The air force says: "Information gained through battlespace characterisation is a valuable foundation to inform targeting."

2. Collection operations are undertaken to acquire raw data and information about relevant aspects of the operational environment. The data and information are passed on to those agencies responsible for

BELOW • *Civilian contractors embarked with the 31st Marine Expeditionary Unit, prepare to conduct a V-BAT drone flight aboard the amphibious dock landing ship USS Rushmore (LSD 47) in the Philippine Sea, on August 24, 2022. The V-BAT is a platform with intelligence, surveillance, and reconnaissance capabilities that requires no launch equipment, making it a useful tool for expeditionary operations.* US MARINE CORPS/LCPL MANUEL ALVARADO

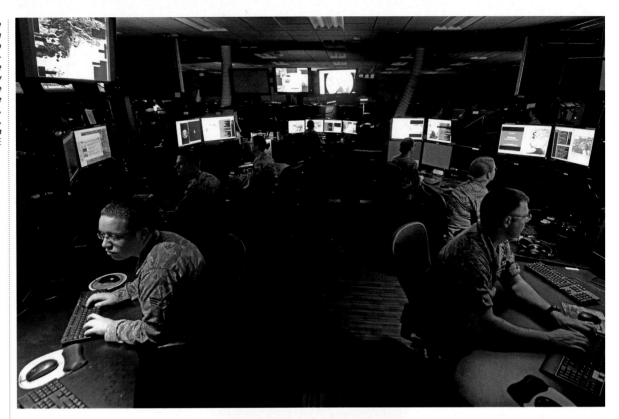

RIGHT • *The Air Force Distributed Common Ground System, also referred to as the GSQ-272 Sentinel, is the US Air Force's primary intelligence, surveillance and reconnaissance collection, processing, exploitation, analysis, and dissemination system.* US AIR FORCE

processing and exploiting the information. The air force says: "Collection involves tasking and synchronising ISR sensors, platforms, and exploitation resources to characterise the operational environment, adversary activities, and infrastructure, and to find, fix, track, and when required, target entities in the battlespace (see below). Its aim is to test beliefs, confirm knowledge, and discover intelligence gaps to enhance the decision-making process. Collection operations are typically driven by battlespace characterisation or targeting requirements."

3. Targeting is the process of selecting and prioritising targets and matching an appropriate response to them, considering operational requirements and capabilities.

Targeting requires expertise of multiple disciplines, and a continuous, analytical process to identify, develop, and affect targets to meet commander objectives. Intelligence is critical for the six-step targeting process: detection, location, identification, decision, execution, and assessment.

Levels of Command

Like all other US Air Force mission sets, ISR is required and conducted by several organisations, each with a commander with individual responsibilities.

Latest Equipment

Ultra-Long Endurance Unmanned Air Platform

The Air Force Research Laboratory's Center for Rapid Innovation (CRI) successfully completed initial flight tests for a revolutionary Unmanned Aerial System (UAS) with a customisable suite of ISR tools that supports extended missions.

Flight testing began at Dugway Proving Ground, Utah, in February 2019 and culminated with a two and a half-day continuous flight demonstration on December 9-11. Subsequent flight tests demonstrated increased levels of flight endurance.

Ultra-LEAP consists of a Pipistrel Sinus sport-class cruiser/glider airframe converted to a fully automated system with autonomous take-off and landing capabilities, an anti-jam GPS, and a satellite-based command and control and high-rate ISR data relay link.

Dr Alok Das, the AFRL's senior scientist said: "Accomplished after only ten months of development by our AFRL/industry team, the two-and-a-half-day mission is a significant milestone in solving the tyranny of distance problem for ISR systems."

A Combatant Commander tasks intelligence forces to achieve national and theatre objectives and has the authority to validate and prioritise requirements for collection by theatre ISR assets.

A Joint Force Commander (JFC) establishes priorities for intelligence operations that align with national and theatre objectives and ensures theatre planning efforts support the fulfilment of crisis intelligence requirements. High priority, time-sensitive requirements are identified and pre-validated by the JFC for the air component commander to consider for dynamic re-tasking during the execution of intelligence operations.

An Air Component Commander is typically the supported commander for theatre ISR and often has delegated responsibility for collection operations and operational control of assigned or attached airborne ISR assets, as delegated by the JFC.

The US Air Force Air Combat Command (ACC) is the lead major command for managing numerous ISR capabilities which it deploys in support of Combatant Commander. Capabilities assigned to ACC include the RC-135 Rivet Joint and U-2S Dragon Lady aircraft (which you can read about in this edition), the Distributed Common Ground System, and cyber-space, geospatial, science and technology, signals and measurement and signature intelligence, all-source analysis, targeting, and associated intelligence products.

Most ISR assets are considered high demand, low density and

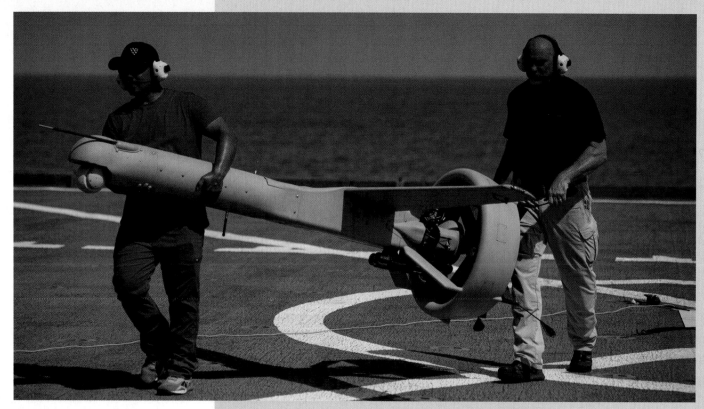

are often tasked to perform a range of missions across the globe in support of Combatant Commanders with an area of responsibility and those with global responsibility.

According to the US Air Force: "It provides JFCs and Air Component Commanders with some intelligence capabilities via reach back, distributed operations, or remote split operations. This enables the employment of ISR capabilities with a reduced, disaggregated forward footprint. Reach back supports forward operations from a rear position, which is often more easily protected and resourced. Similarly, distributed, and remote split operations provide a resiliency benefit by complicating adversary targeting. Despite these benefits, reach back and distributed operations have some limitations: they may limit face-to-face interaction and require significant communications infrastructure to support resilient data processing, exploitation, storage, and other dissemination means."

Remote split operations use forward-deployed, unmanned aerial vehicles operated from a home station via satellite links. This operating model reduces the forward-deployed footprint with most of the mission crews and communications architecture located at a base in the United States or a rear area and enables aircrews to rapidly transition between missions across the globe in response to dynamic and changing

LEFT • *Two civilian contractors embarked with the 31st Marine Expeditionary Unit carry a V-BAT drone aboard the amphibious dock landing ship USS Rushmore (LSD 47) in the Philippine Sea on August 24, 2022.*
US MARINE CORPS/LCPL MANUEL ALVARADO

BELOW • *An F-16C Fighting Falcon assigned to the 555th Expeditionary Fighter Squadron arrives at Al Dhafra Air Base, United Arab Emirates, on July 17, 2023. The aircraft is fitted with an AAQ-33 Sniper targeting pod which captures high-resolution imagery used for intelligence products, as such an F-16 equipped with a Sniper pod is a non-traditional intelligence, surveillance, and reconnaissance asset.*
US AIR FORCE/AIRMAN 1ST CLASS CHRISTIAN SILVERA

requirements. With prior authorisation, Combat Commanders can shift mission crew capacity from one AOR to another when a short-term, excess capacity in the losing AOR results from either weather or maintenance related issues.

Intelligence Process Activities

The joint intelligence process provides the basis for common intelligence terminology and procedures and involves the following eight primary activities.

Planning and Directing

Within the Air Operations Center, the intelligence process begins in strategy development. The ISR strategy is synchronised with theatre and national strategies and defines the roles ISR, and intelligence capabilities will play in achieving operational objectives. Further, it provides the foundation to develop and validate intelligence

requirements, establishes the framework for planning and directing ISR operations, and guides how ISR processes are conducted. During planning, intelligence requirements are determined, appropriate architectures are developed, and collection plans are prepared.

Collection

Collection refers to operations and activities that acquire and provide information to processing personnel by tasking appropriate assets or resources that acquire the data and information required. Collection includes identifying, prioritising, coordinating, and positioning assets or resources to satisfy intelligence requirements. Many airborne ISR assets used in collection can be based or launched from airfields outside an area of interest, enabling collection to be conducted without need for a significant forward footprint, thereby presenting potential

operational advantages in some circumstances.

Processing and Exploitation

Collected data is correlated, converted into a suitable format, and transformed into information that can be readily disseminated, used, exploited, transmitted, stored, and retrieved by intelligence analysts for subsequent analysis and intelligence production. Relevant time-sensitive information about targeting, personnel recovery, or threat warnings produced are immediately disseminated.

Analysis and Production

Processed and exploited data is converted into intelligence by integrating, evaluating, analysing, and interpreting all-source data to produce intelligence products. ISR-generated data can provide an understanding of demographics, culture, physical terrain, centres

Latest Equipment

V-BAT Unmanned Air System

In March 2023, Northrop Grumman teamed with Shield AI, the designer and manufacturer of the V-BAT unmanned air system (UAS) aircraft, was selected by the US Army to participate in the second increment of its Future Tactical Unmanned Aircraft System (FTUAS) competition to replace the RQ-7B Shadow tactical unmanned aerial system.

FTUAS is the US Army's primary vertical take-off and landing unmanned aircraft modernisation effort to provide an expeditionary UAS, capable of persistent aerial reconnaissance for US Army brigade combat teams, special forces, and Ranger battalions.

The team defined a modular open-system architecture for the enhanced V-BAT aircraft, which features increased power and capacity to carry a range of interchangeable and customisable payloads, including electro-optical/infrared sensors, millimetre wave infrared camera, synthetic aperture radar, electronic warfare systems and wide area search AI-based capabilities.

Earlier versions of the V-BAT have supported operations for the US Navy and US Marine Corps

On October 10, 2023, California-based defence technology company Shield AI launched a new drone swarming capability called V-Bat Teams. Shield AI hopes it might be evaluated for the Department of Defense Replicator initiative which seeks to field thousands of autonomous, attritable drones in the next two years to counter the pacing threat posed by China.

V-BAT aircraft are intended to operate autonomously in high-threat environments, without needing instructions or guidance from GPS or communications.

According to Shield AI, the V-BAT aircraft has no exposed rotors or blades and features a ducted fan design, which increases thrust by 80% compared to equivalent engine power and enables take-off and landing with a single engine. The company says the aircraft can fly for 12 hours or hover for hours on end, and its thrust vectoring provides unmatched control authority with stability in harsh weather conditions. The duct adds increased safety, eliminating operator safety zones, which expands the tactical employment envelope.

Shield AI says V-BAT is a tactical asset with strategic applications that is fully deployable by a two-person team and packs up in under 20 minutes to fit in the back of a pickup truck or a UH-60 Blackhawk helicopter. The V-BAT aircraft is designed for runway and equipment-independent launch and recovery from austere locations with no external support.

Software updates are released on a quarterly cycle with a new mission computer released every two years. The mission computer controls functions for visual odometry (the use of data from motion sensors to estimate change in position over time), sensor fusion, localisation and mapping, obstacle detection, and path-planning algorithms.

Shield AI says its V-BAT Teams is scalable to hundreds and even thousands of aircraft, which it says will: "Shift warfare toward large teams of autonomous aircraft that perceive their real-time environment. This capability will unlock intelligent, affordable mass that will overwhelm adversaries through superiority of numbers, saturate area defence systems and force them to waste guided-munition stockpiles and trade them for comparatively cheap [V-BAT] aircraft."

Shield AI conducted the first flight of V-Bat Teams in April and conducted a demonstration as part of the US Air Force AFWERX (see below) autonomy effort in June which showed how the Hivemind technology could launch and autonomously control a trio of V-BATS to monitor, and survey simulated wildfires. The company currently has four V-BAT aircraft, which will increase to eight in 2024, then to 16.

Hivemind's artificial intelligence piloting software for drone swarms can control lots of V-BAT aircraft but the process remains limited by the logistics of launching and then landing multiple aircraft at once.

AFWERX is a US Air Force organisation that brings cutting edge ingenuity from small businesses and start-ups to address the most pressing challenges of the Department of the Air Force.

Brandon Tseng, Shield AI's president said: "Sending large swarms of drones into the air isn't a new trick, as such demonstrations are commonly done at festivals or other celebratory events. Those are brittle, dumb drones that would fall out of the sky or automatically land if they were jammed."

Tseng said the company is initially focussing on maritime domain awareness missions, but V-BATS' could be used to include the suppression of enemy air defences, strike operations, escort missions, logistics operations and as decoys.

Shield AI is marketing the V-BAT Teams concept to the US armed forces and foreign customers.

V-BAT Characteristics

Wingspan	9ft 8in (2.95m)
Length	9ft (2.74m)
Max gross weight	125lb (56kg)
Endurance	10 hours depending on environmental conditions,
Landing zone	12 x 12ft (3.65 x 3.65m)
Max payload	25lb (11kg)
Hover to flight transition	<15 seconds
Service ceiling above MSL	20,000ft

of gravity, financial, social, and political infrastructures. Analysis and production are accomplished through a structured series of actions that typically occur in sequence.

Integration

Information is received, collated, and entered in appropriate databases by analysis and production personnel working in the theatre joint intelligence operations centre. Information is integrated and grouped with related pieces of data according to predetermined criteria to evaluate newly received information.

Evaluation

New information is evaluated by the appropriate analysis and production personnel with a focus on a source's reliability and credibility. To avoid bias, the reliability and credibility of each source is assessed independently.

Analysis

Integrated and evaluated information is compared with known facts and predetermined assumptions to form assessments, which are combined and evaluated to discern patterns, links, or recognised events. Analytical fundamentals typically include the activities of discovery, assessment, explanation, anticipation, and delivery.

Interpretation

Information is judged in relation to existing information and intelligence, which involves identification of new activities and decisions regarding the significance of those activities.

Intelligence Fusion

Execution of the eight steps enables intelligence fusion—a process that examines all sources of intelligence and information to derive a comprehensive assessment of activity. Efforts to produce fused intelligence can be bolstered by establishing collaborative environments and structures to provide access to recognised experts. This is especially important when the units and experts involved are geographically separated.

Advances in network capabilities greatly enhance analysts' ability to share, compare, and assess information. As databases grow in volume and complexity so finding and retrieving information is difficult, consequently virtual knowledge bases have been designed to serve as integrated repositories of multiple databases, reference documents, and open-source material to overcome the difficulties.

Types of Intelligence

Various intelligence methodologies and products are used to provide commanders, staffs, and operational units with predictive analysis, real- and near-real-time threat assessment, and target and friendly forces status. They include:

Warning Intelligence

Warning intelligence products are derived from a worldwide system that analyses and integrates information to assess the probability of hostile actions and provide sufficient warning to pre-empt or counter their effects. Warning intelligence systems rely on information and indications from sources at all levels.

Current Intelligence

Current intelligence is produced by fusing data and intelligence

BELOW • For illustrative purposes only. Space-based intelligence systems are integral to military operations providing information to commanders allowing them to quickly assess the situation and develop concepts of operation. US AIR FORCE

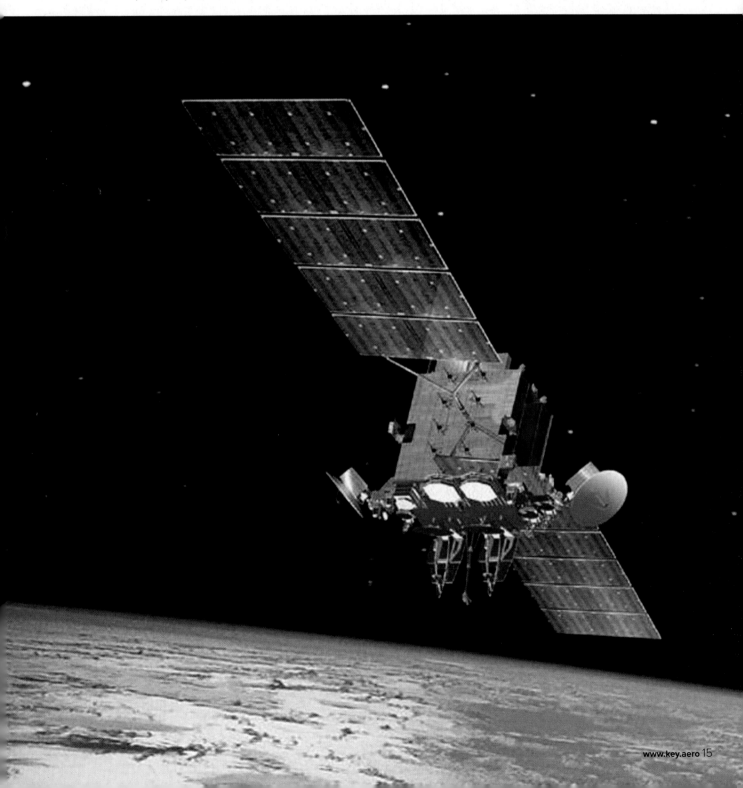

products regarding the current situation in a particular area or the activities of specific groups. Current intelligence requires continuous monitoring of world events and specific activities in an operational area.

General Military Intelligence

General military intelligence (GMI) is all about the military capabilities of foreign nations or topics affecting potential US or multinational military operations. Development of current intelligence forms the basis for the GMI effort and other analytical products. Conversely, GMI provides underlying threat information to produce accurate and meaningful current intelligence.

ABOVE • *The Northrop Grumman RQ-4 Global Hawk high-altitude, long-endurance unmanned aerial vehicle provides lots of data and information used in intelligence products captured by a high-resolution synthetic aperture radar and electro-optical and infrared sensors.* US AIR FORCE/BRYCE BENNETT

LEFT • *The US Air Force fleet of 17 RC-135 Rivet Joint aircraft form the backbone of manned ISR systems providing US commanders with signals and electronic intelligence data and information.* US AIR FORCE/ SENIOR AIRMAN TAYLOR CRUL

Target Intelligence

Intelligence operations play a prominent role in the targeting cycle by detecting, locating, and identifying targets and supporting mission planning and assessment. Target intelligence portrays and locates the components of a target or target complex and indicates its vulnerability and relative importance.

ISR aircraft may be employed to detect and identify potential targets, changes to existing targets, or to conduct battle damage assessment. To support the precision engagement of specific targets, multiple missions may be required to provide the level of detail required.

Scientific and Technical Intelligence

Scientific and technical intelligence (S&TI) examines foreign developments in basic and applied sciences and technologies with potential for military use, particularly to enhance weapon systems. ST&I intelligence is based on the collection, evaluation, analysis, and interpretation of foreign information.

Geospatial Intelligence

Geospatial intelligence (GEOINT) consists of imagery, imagery intelligence (IMINT), and geospatial information. The exploitation and analysis of which helps to describe, assess, and visually depict physical features and geographically referenced activities on or about planet Earth. For example, GEOINT can give a commander the best vantage point for shooters, the most advantageous entry points to the target area.

Intelligence Resources

To conclude the brief overview of the fundamentals of the ISR role it's appropriate to look at the types of resources available to gather data and information.

The US Air Force doctrine publication states how an understanding of intelligence collection resources ensures effective allocation of assets to meet requirements.

Airborne ISR can provide a unique and visible presence to provide real-time, tailorable information during mission execution. All types of aircraft can cover a large area with a mix of sensors, and most are equipped with a common data link between aircraft or ground stations, allowing them to distribute large volumes of information in near-real-time.

Most intelligence missions are flown using standoff techniques when the threat is too significant to allow a high-value ISR asset to enter enemy airspace or when the overflight of an area cannot be completed due to political sensitivities. Range and depth of sensor coverage are limited at stand-off ranges.

If the capacity of traditional ISR-only assets is insufficient to satisfy all collection requirements, resources are not limited to specific platforms or sensors.

All aircraft are capable of conducting reconnaissance or surveillance to varying degrees. Even though ISR is not their primary mission, such aircraft are classed as non-traditional ISR (NTISR) aircraft which can be tasked to provide a wide range of ISR collection support, though availability may be intermittent.

Space-based intelligence systems are integral to military operations providing information to commanders allowing them to quickly assess situations and develop concepts of operation.

Global and wide-area coverage over denied areas where ground and airborne sources are limited, mission longevity and reduced vulnerability to adversary action are the advantages of space-based systems. However, demands on individual space-based systems often exceed capacity, their orbit requirements may limit the ability to meet operational requirements, and adversary denial and deception techniques may limit their functionality.

Equipped with various sensors, space-based military systems provide a range of capabilities and routinely support training exercises, peacekeeping operations, disaster and humanitarian relief efforts, counterterrorism, counterdrug operations, and environmental monitoring.

In support of their military operator, space-based ISR systems provide military forces with geographic and detailed terrain information to enhance mission planning capabilities.

BELOW • *Operating at altitudes over 70,000ft, the otherworldly U-2S Dragon Lady is a reconnaissance aircraft that provides critical imagery to meet the intelligence needs of combatant commanders during peacetime or any phase of conflict.* US AIR FORCE/SENIOR AIRMAN BOBBY CUMMINGS

Reconnaissance Kings and Queens

Mark Ayton reviews the highly specialised Boeing RC-135 reconnaissance aircraft operated by the US Air Force 55th Wing.

Of all the variants of the C-135 aircraft that have served with the US Air Force, the RC-135 Rivet Joint is perhaps the most distinctive with its extended thimble nose and slab-sided cheek fairings.

The US Air Force Rivet Joint fleet comprises eight RC-135Vs (originally built as C-135Bs) and nine RC-135Ws, former RC-135B aircraft.

The 38th and 343rd Reconnaissance Squadrons – part of the 55th Wing - operate the RC-135 Rivet Joint fleet from Offutt AFB in Nebraska to provide near real-time ELINT and COMINT collection, analysis and dissemination capabilities

to US theatre and national chain of command authorities. Providing theatre commanders with ELINT and COMINT data is a tactical role which has been adopted by the Rivet Joint fleet since the end of the Cold War. In the tactical role, the aircraft provide commanders with imminent threat and time-sensitive information about the location and intent of enemy forces. Rivet Joint's capability to broadcast combat advisory information and threat warnings to aircraft in danger has elevated the tactical mission to one with high priority.

An RC-135 flight crew comprises a pilot, co-pilot, and navigator. The aircraft can carry a maximum of 35 passengers

which includes an augmented crew including a pilot, navigator, two crew chiefs and maintenance personnel though numbers and permutations of crew vary.

The RC-135 Rivet Joint is divided into three compartments; the flight deck; the RAVEN compartment which is the forward reconnaissance section used for the ELINT mission; and the operators' compartment which is the aft reconnaissance section used for the COMINT mission.

RAVENS are Electronic Warfare officers who operate the AEELS (Automatic ELINT Emitter Locator System) suite and the manually

BELOW • *An RC-135 Rivet Joint assigned to the 763rd Expeditionary Reconnaissance Squadron taxies off during Exercise Agile Spartan at Naval Support Activity Souda Bay, Crete on August 19, 2023. The RC-135 aircraft participated in Agile Spartan to provide theatre and national level consumers with near real-time, on-scene intelligence collection, analysis, and dissemination capabilities.* US AIR FORCE/SENIOR AIRMAN LEON REDFERN

operated direction-finding antenna. The RAVEN compartment has three consoles designated RAVEN 1, 2 and 3.

RAVEN 1 hosts the tactical co-ordinator and runs the AEELS automatic collection system; RAVEN 2 (the mid console) hosts the tactical co-ordinator - the orchestrator for both the ELINT and COMINT operators; and RAVEN 3 (the forward console) runs the manual collection system.

RAVEN 1 establishes the priorities of scans to search for ELINT activity, resolves emitter ambiguities, performs fine grain measurement of the signal environment, and locates and records signals of interest.

As the tactical co-ordinator, RAVEN 1 is responsible for mission reporting, and for ensuring that the crew is kept informed of the tactical situation and of any changes to the aircraft's collection capability.

RAVEN 1 serves as the reconnaissance commander and manages the crew resources, coordinating with the airborne mission supervisor to correlate COMINT and ELINT data, and to provide time-critical reporting, while overseeing the entire mission crew.

Behind the RAVEN's consoles, the most forward two operator stations are used by Airborne System Engineers (ASEs) who monitor and troubleshoot all the mission systems and undertake light maintenance i.e., the ASEs change components sourced from the spares store located at the aft of the operator's compartment. The ASEs are involved with all aspects of the mission keeping the systems running to enable the complete mission to go, one ASE is dedicated to the ELINT systems and the other to the COMINT systems.

Positioned aft of the ASEs, are consoles used by each of the 12-person cryptologic crew comprising four management positions and eight operator positions.

The furthest forward management position hosts the data link operator (DLO) who oversees all data link operations required to satisfy local, theatre, and national tasking, and co-ordinates with the ELINT compartment to fuse their data with that collected by the cryptologic mission crew.

Next to the DLO is the airborne analyst, who oversees the analysis and reporting effort derived from collection by the cryptologic mission crew and maintains communications networks with national and tactical entities.

LEFT • *A cryptologic language analyst checks his flight mask on an RC-135 Rivet Joint during Operation Agile Spartan at Naval Support Activity Souda Bay, Crete on August 20, 2023. The exercise demonstrated the 379th Air Expeditionary Wing's ability to rapidly generate combat airpower and engage in agile combat employment scenarios.* US AIR FORCE/SENIOR AIRMAN LEON REDFERN

BELOW • *An RC-135 Rivet Joint assigned to the 763rd Expeditionary Reconnaissance Squadron, taxies to the runway at Naval Support Activity Souda Bay, Crete, on August 20, 2023, during Exercise Agile Spartan.* US AIR FORCE/SENIOR AIRMAN LEON REDFERN

Next to the airborne analyst is the airborne mission supervisor (AMS), the senior cryptologic authority on the aircraft, who oversees the cryptologic mission crew's collection and reporting activities and liaises with RAVEN 2.

Next to the AMS is the information integration officer (IIO), who oversees the co-ordination of all-source intelligence real time via SIPRNET chat and web communications systems on and off the aircraft, who has top secret or sensitive compartmented information clearance.

Eight airborne cryptologic language analysts, all of whom are linguists, work at consoles behind the four management positions: the first three

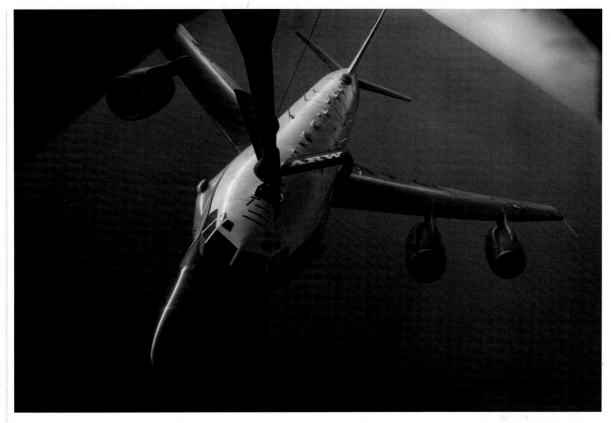

RIGHT • *An RC-135 Rivet Joint assigned to the 763rd Expeditionary Reconnaissance Squadron receives fuel from a KC-135 Stratotanker assigned to the 912th Expeditionary Air Refueling Squadron during Operation Agile Spartan above the US Central Command's area of responsibility on August 19, 2023.* US AIR FORCE/SENIOR AIRMAN LEON REDFERN

BELOW • *An RC-135 Rivet Joint assigned to the 95th Reconnaissance Squadron, taxies on the flightline to begin the first hot-pit refuelling mission for the airframe at Royal Air Force Mildenhall, England on August 14, 2023. Hot-pit refuelling can enable the RC-135 to perform an operational mission, recover to an airfield for refuelling, then perform another mission without the use of a power cart.* US AIR FORCE/AIRMAN 1ST CLASS CHRISTOPHER CAMPBELL

are classed as lead operators, with the remainder categorised as cryptologic operators.

Two positions further aft host a signals search and development operator - a special signals analyst (not a linguist) who searches the frequency spectrum for new (mainly non-voice) signals, new or unusual emitters or communications systems – and a reconnaissance, surveillance, target acquisition (RSTA) operator (a linguist or a special signals' operator), who works known, non-voice, digital data systems.

In the early days of Rivet Joint operations, these crew members were drawn from dedicated US Air Force Security Service squadrons, while the flight crew and RAVENs were drawn from the 55th Strategic Reconnaissance Wing's operational squadrons, such that on a given mission, an RC-135's crew would come from two different units, reporting to different chains of command.

During a mission, the ELINT operators will pick up a signal and,

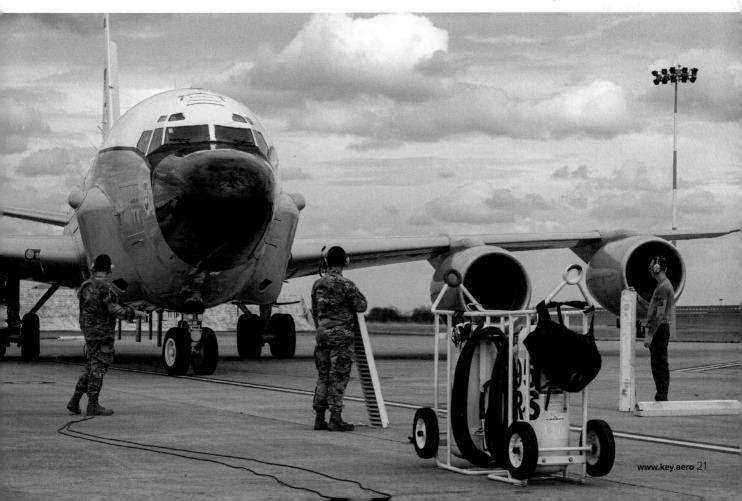

as explained by RAVEN crew to the author, initially identify it as a Coke, then once analysis has been conducted the identity can be refined to a diet Cherry Coke. All intercepted signals' data is retained and can be sent to the CAOC via satellite, datalink, and radio communications. This data transfer capability makes the Rivet Joint a near real time data provider to the CAOC.

Each RAVEN console has an upper and lower BARCO screen. The upper screen has a map display for situational awareness used to identify potential hostiles. The lower screen is used to interface between systems and monitor the ELINT equipment.

The RAVEN computer system integrates the ELINT data collected to complete the Rivet Joint mission.

Pacer Crag Flight Deck

As the Rivet Joint aircraft entered Program Depot Maintenance (PDM) during the early 2000s, they were fitted with the C-135 Pacer Crag glass cockpit and General Electric F108 (CFM56-2B-1) turbofan engines. The reworked aircraft are GATM qualified and RVSM capable. The upgrade provides each pilot with one multi-function display on the right of the console and a partial-function display on the left.

Each Rivet Joint aircraft is equipped with: GPS/INS; Doppler radar; and a Flight Management System (FMS) which is run off the LN100 inertial GPS system. The LN100 drives the navigational systems and the FMS and FM immunity radios. A weather radar on the navigator's position is used for ground mapping. All operator consoles are fitted with BARCO flat screen monitors.

Rivet Joint crew told the author how the improved layout of the upgraded aircraft lead to better crew comfort not to mention better cabin lighting. Equipped with more powerful computers, the upgraded aircraft has an enhanced mission capability, completing an increased number of tasks, because of the increased computing power and improved mission equipment.

Crew comfort was considerably improved with the new F108 (CFM56-2B-1) turbofan engines. The air-conditioned environment within the rear cabin of the RC-135 is so efficient that the cabin can now become so cold that aircrew are forced to wear flight jackets.

The Rivet Joint can take off with a heavier fuel load and high air temperatures are less of an inhibitor because each F108 engine provides 21,000lb of thrust compared to the 16,500lb provided by the TF33. This effects the pilot's technique during take-off and landing. "Because the new engine pods are closer to the ground, the pilot has to watch out for pitch, bank angle and landing speed to avoid scrapping the pods, especially on landing on a crowned runway," one RJ pilot explained.

Despite these handling characteristics, there have been no changes made to the technical orders governing the aircraft's handling limitations.

Rivet Joint Systems

The RC-135 Rivet Joint cheek fairings house some of the primary Electronic INTelligence (ELINT) side-facing antennas integrated with the Automatic ELINT Emitter Locator System (AEELS). To undertake the full SIGINT mission,

Rivet Joint needs the capability to collect signals from across the entire electromagnetic spectrum. AEELS is the primary system used to gather those signals, process them, and filter out the most significant and interesting. Selected signals are then served to the onboard operator stations for analysis by the system operators. Mission data is recorded on computer hard drives. A laser jet printer is carried to provide a hard copy print out of the collated ELINT and COMINT data.

Seven RC-135Cs were converted to the RC-135V-configuration fitted with the AEELS system, followed by six RC-135Ms converted to the RC-135W-configuration. All the RC-135Ws were fitted with the TF33-V9 engine. The entire conversion programme was undertaken to enable all aircraft to undertake a joint SIGINT mission, which is where the Rivet Joint name is partly derived from.

In 1976, the first Rivet Joint aircraft, RC-135V 64-14848, was fitted with the fully automated MUltiple position COMINT Emitter Location System (MUCELS), which is a standard system throughout the fleet used to collect communication intelligence across a wide frequency band. The most visible component of the MUCELS system is the 'antenna farm' of large plate aerials, on the fuselage underside.

All Rivet Joints have satellite communication links, which are facilitated by seven T-shaped aerials fitted on the top of the fuselage.

There are few external differences between the RC-135V and RC-135W, the W-model does however have longer fairings than the RC-135V.

BELOW • *An RC-135 Rivet Joint assigned to the 95th Reconnaissance Squadron, undergoes the first hot-pit refuelling at Royal Air Force Mildenhall, England on August 14, 2023. The hot-pit refuelling was conducted by personnel assigned to the 95th Reconnaissance Squadron and the 100th Air Refueling Wing.* US AIR FORCE/AIRMAN 1ST CLASS CHRISTOPHER CAMPBELL

the pilot. Each receives taskings from the headquarters and mission planning personnel, but these taskings may not be the same signal collects. During the mission brief priority is given to the most important collects so that a compromise is agreed between where the aircraft commander can safely take the aircraft and the needs of both the tactical co-ordinator and the AMS.

During combat operations in Kosovo, Afghanistan, and Iraq, the Rivet Joint played a huge role in the entire battle plan, in the words of one pilot "not just our mission but everyone's mission."

Rivet Joint crew arrive for the brief, given by senior 55th Wing staff, two and a half hours before take-off. On a combat mission the crew will speak with fighter aircrew as part of the multirole operation and intelligence officers to ensure the plan passes what is colloquially known as 'the sanity check' and meets the goal in a safe way.

Once the crew arrive at the aircraft, they work through the pre-flight checklist which usually takes an hour to complete. During this stage of the mission, some systems are not run because they generate too much heat on the ground which affects the avionics and computer systems. Those systems remain shut down until the aircraft reaches cooler air at altitude.

During Operation Iraqi freedom, missions lasting 16-hours were common. Aerial refuelling played

ABOVE • A US Air Force U-2 Dragon Lady takes off in the distance behind an RC-135V Rivet Joint during Dragon Flag East at Offutt Air Force Base, Nebraska. Note the stylised engine covers on the Rivet Joint featuring the aircraft's serial number, Rivet Joint name, and badge of the 55th Aircraft Maintenance Squadron. US AIR FORCE/ LIEUTENANT HAILEY MALAY

BELOW • Pilots taxi an RC-135 Rivet Joint in preparation for launch during Exercise Dragon Flag East at Offutt Air Force Base, Nebraska, on April 1, 2023. US AIR FORCE/2ND LT HAILEY MALAY

Rivet Joint is a platform with a lot of communication capability. Perhaps the most significant installed is the Tactical Digital Information Link (TADIL/A), which enables Rivet Joint to transfer the collated and refined ELINT data to E-3 AWACS aircraft airborne in the theatre of operations. Onboard satellite links enable the ELINT data to be transferred to national chain of command users or onto the near real-time Tactical Information Broadcast Service (TIBS) for use by theatre commanders.

One of the most striking, yet reassuring instruments shown to the author and carried by the RC-135 is the sextant, which is used as a manual back-up for navigational purposes. Rivet Joint crew told the author how it is regularly used during flights crossing the Atlantic and Pacific oceans. The aircraft has a sextant port located in the top of the cabin above the navigator's position.

Rivet Joint Operations

The author spoke with Rivet Joint crew about mission generation and operations. A pilot explained how the respective taskings of the chief electronic warfare officer (the tactical co-ordinator) and the chief enlisted position (the AMS) are of concern to

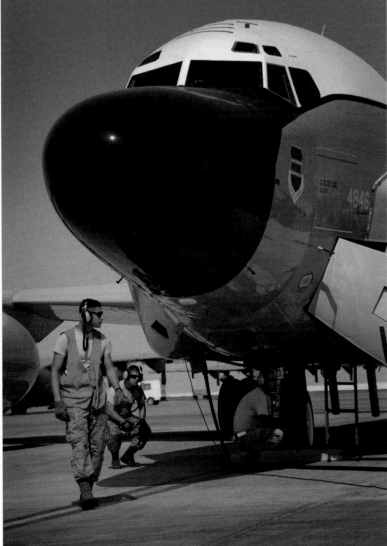

a crucial part of the missions. After departure, with as much fuel load onboard as possible, the Rivet Joint crew would head to the operating area and conduct a scheduled aerial refuelling to bring the aircraft up to 'max tanks', this would enable the aircraft to 'spin around' for up to 12 hours before taking on more fuel to enable the Rivet Joint to safely recover to base.

Whilst 'spinning around', a term used by Rivet Joint crew for loitering in an orbit, certain types of patterns are flown. The pattern tracks are set up during the mission planning and briefing stage and are determined by the mission requirements of the tactical co-ordinator and the AMS. Rivet Joint crew told the author that the SIGINT mission does not require the aircraft to be flown in a 'figure-of-eight' orbit, though this is preferred so that the operators can keep the sensors on the target. The task can be completed on a straight heading depending on how large the area to be swept is.

Decisions on where around the world the Rivet Joint will operate is decided upon at the Pentagon by four-star generals and theorists based largely on where they think the capability

ABOVE • *Airmen assigned to the 379th Expeditionary Aircraft Maintenance Squadron pull an air hose from a RC-135 Rivet Joint at Al Udeid Air Base, Qatar. Cool cabin air is essential for aircraft systems and aircrew when operating at hot locations like Al Udeid Air Base.* US AIR FORCE/SENIOR AIRMAN MILES WILSON

LEFT • *Airmen assigned to the 379th Expeditionary Aircraft Maintenance Squadron pull the chocks of a RC-135 Rivet Joint at Al Udeid Air Base, Qatar.* US AIR FORCE/SENIOR AIRMAN MILES WILSON

is needed the most. The 55th Wing does not have a say in where it deploys, the only influence held by the 55th is in relation to high crew deployment demand.

The 55th Wing has its own deployment cycle doctrine because it has so few aircraft, which must all regularly return to Offutt for routine maintenance based on engine and airframe hours. All Rivet Joint aircraft deployed to the Far East, Europe and Southwest Asia are owned by the in-theatre commanders. A 55th Wing commander is sent to all detachment locations, who runs the operation based on the directives and taskings of the higher command.

The 55th does not stand an alert with the Rivet Joint force but can do so when required.

Alert procedures will be initiated by the applicable squadron commander or detachment commander (DETCO) when mission requirements require a quick response to higher headquarter taskings. The applicable squadron commander or DETCO is the waiver/modification authority for alert procedures, of which there are two different types: Alpha alert and Bravo alert.

When holding an Alpha alert, the Rivet Joint aircrew can launch within one hour of crew notification. Crews are quartered near the alert aircraft with sufficient transportation to launch in accordance with mission timing. Crew members are given 12-hours of pre-alert crew rest.

When holding a Bravo alert, the Rivet Joint aircrew can launch within four hours of crew notification. Crew members are given 12-hours of pre-

alert crew rest. After crew rest, they are placed on telephone standby.

A crew will not stay on alert duty for more than 48 hours, after which they must be launched, released, or entered in pre-departure crew rest. Crew duty begins when the person in charge is notified of the launch order.

Ground Maintenance

The maintenance squadron is responsible for the airframe, the engines, landing gear, hydraulics, electrics, power systems, air systems, the cockpit systems, and structural elements within the rear compartments.

A Rivet Joint maintenance crew comprises three crew chiefs and one maintainer for each speciality (hydraulic systems, communications/navigation systems, guidance control, electrical and environmental systems, electronic warfare systems and engines) - nine people in total.

A crew chief assigned to the maintenance squadron told the author that to put an RC-135 Rivet Joint into the air, on average, takes 20-hours of work for the crew chief alone. Each Rivet Joint mission requires approximately 60-man hours of pre-flight preparation from the maintenance crew and commences eight hours prior to the planned take-off time assuming the aircraft is already on the ground and fuelled.

The pre-flight inspection check takes six hours to complete covering accumulators for the hydraulic systems, tyre pressures, onboard oxygen quantities, correct fuel load, panel inspection, engine inspection,

inspection for leaks, cabin preparation, and cleaning.

The work required at the end of a mission is similarly extensive and lasts for as long as it takes to fix the maintenance write-ups. The inspection and refuelling lasts between three and four hours covering post-flight inspection, a check for bird damage and loss of components, a check of tires and brakes for wear, refuelling, and to fix the maintenance write-ups.

Crew Training and TC-135W Trainers

The 338th Combat Training Squadron trains RC-135 pilots, navigators, RAVENS, and operators and is known colloquially as a nose-to-tail training unit. Pilots come direct from pilot training and take between six and nine months to achieve combat mission capability depending on the availability of jets on which to train. Navigators arrive fully trained and receive SNO training with an instructor navigator.

RAVEN operators go through navigator school with combat systems specialisation with the 479th Flying Training Group at Naval Air Station Pensacola, Florida. The course lasts one year using T-6A Texan II and T-1A Jayhawk aircraft. Once the students have completed the course at Pensacola they are sent to Offutt and join the 338th Combat Training Squadron (CTS) which is the formal training unit for the RAVEN crewmembers.

RAVENS take one year to train before they are combat mission

BELOW • *An RC-135 Rivet Joint assigned to the 379th Air Expeditionary Wing takes off at Al Udeid Air Base, Qatar, on a reconnaissance in support of Operation Inherent Resolve.* US AIR FORCE/SENIOR AIRMAN MILES WILSON

55th Wing RC-135 Fleet

RC-135S Cobra Ball	Details
61-2662	c/n 18292. Converted to RC-135S in 1983.
61-2663	c/n 18333. Converted to RC-135S in 1969.
62-4128 Cobra Ball 2	c/n 18468. Converted from RC-135X to RC-135S in 1989.
RC-135U Combat Sent	
64-14847	c/n 18787. Converted from RC-135C to RC-135U in 1971.
64-14849	c/n 18789. Converted from RC-135C to RC-135U.
RC-135V Rivet Joint	
63-9792	c/n 18787. Converted from RC-135U to RC-135V in 1986-1987.
64-14841	c/n 18781. Converted from RC-135C to RC-135V in 1975.
64-14842	c/n 18782. Converted from RC-135C to RC-135V in 1973.
64-14843	c/n 18783. Converted from RC-135C to RC-135V in 1973.
64-14844	c/n 18784. Converted from RC-135C to RC-135V.
64-14845	c/n 18785. Converted from RC-135C to RC-135V in 1974-1975.
64-14846	c/n 18786. Converted from RC-135C to RC-135V in 1991.
64-14848	c/n 18788. Converted from RC-135C to RC-135V.
RC-135W Rivet Joint	
62-4125	c/n 18465. Converted from C-135B to RC-135W.
62-4126	c/n 18466. Converted from C-135B to RC-135W.
62-4130	c/n 18470. Converted from C-135B to RC-135W.
62-4131	c/n 18471. Converted from RC-135M to RC-135W in 2006.
62-4132	c/n 18472. Converted from RC-135M to RC-135W in 1984.
62-4134	c/n 18474. Converted from RC-135M to RC-135W in 1981.
62-4135	c/n 18475. Converted from RC-135M to RC-135W in 2001.
62-4138	c/n 18478. Converted from RC-135M to RC-135W in 1978.
62-4139	c/n 18479. Converted from RC-135M to RC-135W in 1984-1985.
TC-135W Trainer	
62-4127	c/n 18467. Converted from C-135B to TC-135W.
62-4129	c/n 18469. Converted from C-135B to TC-135W.
62-4133	c/n 18473. Converted from TC-135S to TC-135W.

ABOVE • *An RC-135 Rivet Joint assigned to the 379th Air Expeditionary Wing moves from its parking spot at Al Udeid Air Base, Qatar.* US AIR FORCE/SENIOR AIRMAN MILES WILSON

With a current fleet of just 17 aircraft and a constant worldwide demand for Rivet Joint capabilities, familiarisation, and conversion training on one of the 17 aircraft is not easily justified. Consequently, the 55th Wing operates three former C-135B aircraft configured as TC-135W trainers to simulate Rivet

capable and 'ready to go to the fight'. Where real world situation allows, most system operators are trained on the various Rivet Joint sensors during operational missions. A dedicated Rivet Joint Mission Trainer provides a very realistic signal environment in which student operators can train.

The 338th CTS also run instructor upgrades under the Pilot Upgrade Programme. The upgrade programme trains co-pilots to become aircraft commanders and aircraft commanders to become instructor pilots. The Instructor Upgrade Programme also manages the upgrade of navigators, RAVENs, operators, and tactical co-ordinators to become instructors. All student instructors are selected based on specific criteria.

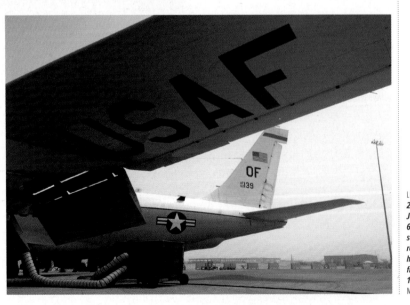

LEFT • *Back in March 2010, RC-135W Rivet Joint, serial number 62-4139 was only the second of its kind to reach 50,000 flight hours since the airframe first took flight in 1962.* US AIR FORCE/TSGT MICHELLE LARCHE

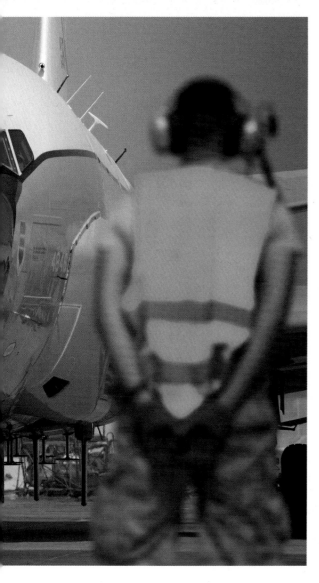

645th Aeronautical Systems Group known as the Big Safari programme office uses an agile incremental baseline upgrade acquisition strategy to introduce new equipment and capabilities to the 17 Rivet Joint, three Cobra Ball, two Combat Sent and Constant Phoenix aircraft.

This strategy provides regular incremental upgrades to meet emerging operational requirements – all set against the background of an evolving threat environment and technologically agile targets and helps to address obsolescence issues and diminishing manufacturing sources (DMS) concerns.

RC-135 aircraft enter Program Depot Maintenance (PDM) every four years for inspection, maintenance, and upgrades undertaken by L-3 Communications at its Greenville, Texas facility under the oversight of the Big Safari programme office.

Baseline content is typically defined from 18 to 36 months prior to fielding, and equipment required for integration in a given baseline upgrade is contracted and purchased in the first year of the procurement funding cycle for acquisition and installation in the following year. This has resulted in a 36 to 48-month interval between the initial operating capability dates of successive baselines. Any technology or capability gaps that emerge can still be addressed via quick reaction capability upgrades.

Baseline upgrades have sometimes resulted in visual differences between different aircraft standards, as well as improvements in capability. Baseline 6, for example, saw the installation of a distinctive radome for the Condor CS-2010 spinning antenna beneath the rear fuselage, while Baseline 7 featured a fin top JTIDS/TADIL-J communications antenna assembly. This fin tip ball was originally intended to serve a wide-band system called Airborne Information Transmission (ABIT), which did not go into service.

Baseline 8 aircraft had their distinctive under-fuselage MUCELS antennas replaced by plain blade antennas, which serve the new Search, Radar, Direction Finding (SRDF) system. Three under-nose blade antennas also disappeared at this time.

Joint. Each TC-135W aircraft has the thimble nose and mock side cheeks but is not fitted with mission equipment.

Baseline Upgrades

To exploit the rapid evolution of both COTS (commercial off-the-shelf) and bespoke technologies, the US Air Force

RIGHT • *Airmen connect an air hose to an RC-135 Rivet Joint at Al Udeid Air Base, Qatar to provide cool air in the cabin, helping aircrew and avionics systems.* US AIR FORCE/TSGT MICHELLE LARCHE

FAR RIGHT • *Airmen complete aircraft forms for maintenance on an autopilot system.* US AIR FORCE/TSGT MICHELLE LARCHE

LEFT • *RC-135V, serial number 64-14844/ OF, assigned to the 95th Reconnaissance Squadron lands at RAF Mildenhall, Suffolk on September 5, 2023.* MARK AYTON

Baseline 9 introduced a new under-floor liquid-cooling system which necessitated the installation of radiators in the forward part of each AEELS 'cheek', with a new intake and exhaust also in the forward part of the cheeks.

Baseline 10 aircraft are distinguished by a new antenna in a dorsal hump, serving a wideband global satellite (WGS) communications system. The high frequency probes above the outer wings also disappeared with Baseline 10.

In its FY2020 US Air Force budget estimates document published in March 2019, the Department of Defense listed details about the upgrades underway for Cobra Ball, Combat Sent and Rivet Joint aircraft.

All three programmes are managed under an incremental baseline upgrade acquisition strategy to maintain collection parity with evolving and emerging adversarial weapons systems utilised by state and non-state actors. Big Safari's operational requirements document addresses airframe, sensor, navigation, communications, data link, and processing requirements necessary to keep each type of RC-135 and WC-135 aircraft viable through 2050.

Ongoing funding acquires and installs various upgrade and enhancement modifications for all three RC-135 types.

Cobra Ball funding concentrates on the initiatives to complete the development, integration, and fielding of Cobra Ball Baseline 7 enhancements. Subsystem upgrades comprise Foreign Instrumentation Signature INTelligence (FISINT) direction finding and digital data recording, digital search, and target discrimination via SATCOM, and the integration of the Rivet Joint Baseline 11/Baseline 12 communications intelligence suite.

Combat Sent funding concentrates the sustainment and completion of the Combat Sent Baseline 5 and Baseline 6 enhancements. Baseline 6 subsystem upgrades comprise: wideband collection, scientific and technical processors, improved antennas, improved operator interface and reporting tools, sensor calibration/ testing systems, integration of the Rivet Joint Baseline 12 and Baseline 13 communication intelligence (COMINT) suite and enhancing capabilities in dense signal environments. These initiatives formed the basis for the RC-135U Combat Sent fleet modification strategy.

Rivet Joint funding concentrates on sustainment of the fielded Rivet Joint Baseline 12 configured

BELOW • *RC-135W, serial number 62-4131/ OF, assigned to the 95th Reconnaissance Squadron taxies from runway 28 at RAF Mildenhall, Suffolk in October.* MARK AYTON

HOME OF THE FIGHTIN' 55TH

Offutt Air Force Base, Nebraska, is home of the Headquarters of US Strategic Command and the US Air Force 55th Wing, known as the Fightin' 55th, Air Combat Command's largest wing.

Dating back to Fort Crook in 1894, Offutt Field was named in honour of Lieutenant Jarvis Offutt, Omaha's first air casualty of World War One, killed in France on May 10, 1924, whilst flying with the Royal Flying Corps.

From January 1942, Offutt Field was a major production plant of the Glenn L Martin Company where 1,585 B-26 Marauders and 531 B-29 Superfortress were built by the end of World War Two.

Offutt Field became Offutt Air Force Base on January 13, 1948, following the formation of the Unites States Air Force in September 1947. Its most prominent role commenced on November 9, 1948, with the activation of Headquarters, Strategic Air Command (SAC) which remained resident at Offutt until June 1, 1992, when the command was disestablished.

The Fightin' 55th arrived at Offutt during August 1966 from Forbes Air Force Base, Kansas as the then 55th Strategic Reconnaissance Wing (SRW), Strategic Air Command's primary reconnaissance unit. Over

25-years later, on September 1, 1991, the 55th SRW was redesignated as the 55th Wing to reflect the range of reconnaissance and command and control missions undertaken including those flown by the RC-135 Cobra Ball and Cobra Eye equipped 24th Reconnaissance Squadron based at Eareckson Air Force Base, Shemya, Alaska, which were transferred to the 45th RS in 1994. On June 1, 1992, SAC was disestablished and the 55th SRW was transferred to the new Air Combat Command.

Today, flying operations are managed by the 55th Operations Group, the largest in ACC with 2,900 personnel assigned to 11 squadrons and two detachments. A fleet of 27 aircraft including all RC-135, TC-135, WC-135 and the E-4B National Airborne Operations Center aircraft are assigned to the 55th Wing.

The Fightin' 55th has supported every US operation since the end of the Cold War - Southern Watch, Provide Comfort, Vigilant Warrior, Enduring Freedom, and Iraqi Freedom (Southwest Asia), Provide Promise, Deny Flight, (Bosnia-Herzegovina), Support Democracy, Uphold Democracy (Haiti), Tiger Rescue (Yemen), Allied Force (Kosovo), and daily missions in the European Command area of operations related to the war in Ukraine.

55th Wing RC-135 Squadrons

38th Reconnaissance Squadron 'Fighting Hellcats'

The first squadron to move to Offutt in August 1966. Initially it operated SAC's EC-135 Looking Glass mission until April 2, 1970, when the mission was transferred to another unit and the squadron stood down. The then, 38th Strategic Reconnaissance Squadron reactivated on October 26, 1979, as a RC-135 Rivet Joint squadron which it continues to operate today. It was redesignated as a standard Reconnaissance Squadron on September 1, 1991.

45th Reconnaissance Squadron 'Sylvester'

A former RF-4C Phantom squadron (the 45th Tactical Reconnaissance Training Squadron) based at Bergstrom Air Force Base, Texas between April 1, 1982, and September 30, 1989. The 45th was reactivated as a Reconnaissance Squadron at Offutt Air Force Base on July 1, 1994, initially absorbing the RC-135 Cobra Ball and Cobra Eye missions. Today, the 45th RS operates the RC-135S Cobra Ball, RC-135U Combat Sent and the WC-135R Constant Phoenix missions.

82nd Reconnaissance Squadron

Reactivated on October 2, 1991, at Kadena Air Base, Okinawa as a standalone unit assigned to the 55th Operations Group and responsible for RC-135 aircraft and aircrew within the Pacific Air Forces command theatre of operations.

95th Reconnaissance Squadron

Former U-2 squadron assigned to the 17th Reconnaissance Wing based at RAF Alconbury, Cambridgeshire and then the 9th Reconnaissance Wing based at Beale Air Force Base, California until its deactivation on September 15, 1993. The 95th RS was reactivated at RAF Mildenhall, Suffolk on July 1, 1994, as a standalone unit assigned to the 55th Operations Group and responsible for RC-135 aircraft and aircrew within the United States Air Forces Europe command theatre of operations. The squadron also commands Detachment 1 at Naval Support Facility, Souda Bay, Crete.

343rd Reconnaissance Squadron

The original RC-135 Rivet Joint squadron, the 343rd SRS commenced operations at Offutt in 1967 and continues to fly the aircraft today.

During 2003, the 38th and 343rd Reconnaissance Squadrons became similar operational flying squadrons. Prior to the change, the 343rd RS was a RAVEN (Electronic Warfare Officer) squadron, meaning all 55th Wing RAVENS were assigned to the 343rd. The sister squadron, the 38th RS had all the Rivet Joint flight crew assigned and was the operational RC-135V/W squadron. The assets of both squadrons were split and assigned between the 38th and 343rd to enable each to function as a fully operational squadron.

338th Combat Training Squadron

In September 1999 the 338th Combat Training Squadron was activated as a dedicated initial, difference, requalification, and upgrade training squadron for Rivet Joint, Combat Sent, Cobra Ball and Constant Phoenix crew. The squadron manages six different training programmes for reconnaissance, command and control, and treaty verification missions.

aircraft. Baseline 12 subsystem upgrades comprise: precision multi-angle direction finding communications intelligence (DF COMINT) capability, electronic intelligence (ELINT) recorder expansion, precision ELINT digital signals intelligence system integration, wideband global satellite enhanced integration, increased near real time national tactical integration, improved operator interface and reporting tools, enhancing capabilities in dense signal environments (search-through-interference improvement), re-double copy channel count, increased digital signal exploitation, increased digital signal recorder bandwidth, specific emitter ID improvement, enhanced spatial processing/exploitation, Air Force Distributed Common Ground System interoperability, operator work station 3D map projection, enhanced operator reporting management tools, modernised communications security

communications security protocols, continued CNS/ATM compliant cockpit avionics enhancements to include addressing any obsolescence issues, new steerable beam antenna,

enhanced weather radar, and digitally enhanced electronic flight instrument system.

In addition, the funding will ensure integration and fielding of upgraded RC-135 ground systems to include the Rivet Joint Mission Trainer, Ground Data Processing Systems, Distributed Mission Shelters, Mission Crew Training Systems, Airborne Capabilities Extension System, and Operational Flight Trainers.

The ground systems are upgraded to remain consistent with the fielded aircraft configurations to allow for training and qualification of the aircrew and maintenance personnel assigned, plus verification and certification of software builds that are continuously modified to address the dynamic mission requirements of these weapons systems.

This baseline upgrade approach has provided a relatively rapid upgrade

LEFT • *An RC-135 assigned to the 379th Air Expeditionary Wing approaches a KC-135 Stratotanker assigned to the 91st Expeditionary Air Refueling Squadron. It was to receive fuel during an Exercise Juniper Oak mission, within the U.S. Central Command area of responsibility on January 25, 2023. Juniper Oak is a bilateral exercise between US and Israeli armed forces.* US AIR FORCE/TSGT DANIEL ASSELTA

LEFT • *An RC-135 seconds from contact with the aerial refuelling probe extended from a KC-135 Stratotanker assigned to the 91st Expeditionary Air Refueling Squadron.* US AIR FORCE/TSGT DANIEL ASSELTA

BELOW • *An RC-135 Rivet Joint takes-off from Nellis Air Force Base, Nevada for a Weapons School Integration (WSINT) mission.* US AIR FORCE/WILLIAM LEWIS

drumbeat, such that Baseline 1 was introduced in 1990, and Baseline 14 is being defined.

Ongoing Duty

The Rivet Joint continues to provide the backbone of the US Air Force's stand-off, medium-altitude, intelligence-gathering capability. It will be the only dedicated, manned airborne SIGINT platform and MASINT collection system in the US inventory, once the US Navy's EP-3E ARIES II is retired. As it stands, no replacement for the RC-135 aircraft, nor for the capabilities it offers, is in sight. Current planning envisages keeping the RC-135 in service until 2050.

Optical Snoopers

An overview of the unique RC-135S Cobra Ball.

All aircraft assigned to the 55th Wing are unique and special, none more so than three RC-135S Cobra Ball TELemetry INTelligence (TELINT) aircraft flown by the 45th Reconnaissance Squadron.

Cobra Ball's unique mission was originally to monitor Soviet missile activity during the Cold War when the type operated from bases in the western Pacific, primarily Eareckson Air Force Base, Shemya in Alaska. Their task was to collect signature telemetry data of Soviet ballistic missiles and missile re-entry vehicles launched on test. The data collected was analysed to determine the capabilities of each missile.

In the post-Cold War world, Cobra Ball continues to be tasked by the Joint Chiefs of Staff in the TELINT role to collect optical and electronic data from tracking ballistic missile systems and re-entry vehicles for treaty verification in what are termed 'rest-of-world activities', China, India, and Pakistan for example. Cobra Ball is also tasked with spotting battlefield missiles, in the so-called theatre missile defence role. The latter role having been adopted in response to the Scud missile threat faced during Operation Desert Storm in 1991.

RC-135S Cobra Ball

A Cobra Ball flight crew consists of two pilots and two navigators, the mission crew comprises five electronic warfare officers, two in-flight maintenance technicians and six other mission specialists, many of whom are also qualified for the Rivet Joint and Combat Sent missions.

Each RC-135S is configured with a 'thimble' nose, cheek fairings housing electronic receivers, and an aft fuselage teardrop-shaped antenna fairing. The RC-135S nose houses an enhanced weather radar which is used to provide very accurate positional data to the crew, which ensures that during TELINT missions, the crew stay within international airspace. The Cobra Ball radar has a very effective tracking capability, which is used to detect missiles, cruise missiles or aircraft in the Theatre Missile Defence role. The radar tracks the target and provides positional data in a three-dimensional mode in all weather conditions.

Cobra Ball Systems

The most notable modifications on a RC-135S are large circular windows in the starboard fuselage. These facilitate telescopic monitoring devices, advanced optics, and infrared telescopes and sensors used for tracking ballistic-missile tests at long range to provide missile treaty

RIGHT • *An RC-135S Cobra Ball at Offutt Air Force Base, Nebraska. Note the black starboard wing, an attribute that prevents reflection and therefore disturbance to the TELINT system.* US AIR FORCE/ JOSH PLUEGER

BELOW • *An RC-135S Cobra Ball taxies to the runway for take-off at Offutt Air Force Base, Nebraska.* US AIR FORCE/JOSH PLUEGER

verification data and theatre air defence warning.

The two original Cobra Ball aircraft, serial numbers 61-2662 and 61-2663, are equipped with the full SIGnals INTelligence (SIGINT) and Measurement And Signatures INTelligence (MASINT) sensor suites to gather intelligence data from the entire electromagnetic spectrum. Two sided electro-optical/infrared radiometric sensors, infrared telescopes, and spectral sensors called the Real Time Optical System (RTOS) and the Large Aperture Tracker System (LATS) form the MASINT sensor suite.

RTOS is a long-range sensor system, which can acquire, track and record targets in the visible and infrared spectrums. The RTOS staring sensors centred off the wings provide a target acquisition capability with a 120-degree arc on both sides of the aircraft. LATS is an optical telescope, which captures long-range targets in fine-resolution imagery with its 305mm (12-inch) focal length.

Cobra Ball is also equipped with the Medium-wave InfraRed Array (MIRA) optical surveillance sensor (camera) system. MIRA cameras, fitted on both sides of the aircraft, capture missile re-entry imagery within the medium wave infrared spectrum. The MIRA system provides Cobra Ball with an advanced scientific and technical

ABOVE • *RC-135S Cobra Ball, serial number 61-2662, assigned to the 45th Reconnaissance Squadron takes off from Offutt Air Force Base, Nebraska. Note the black starboard wing and engine cowlings, and three windows in the forward fuselage, installed to enable the TELINT system to function.* US AIR FORCE/SENIOR AIRMAN JACOB SKOVO

intelligence collection capability used for foreign ballistic missile system analysis and treaty verification.

The Cobra Ball aircraft have received Joint Tactical Information Distribution System (JTIDS) datalinks and real-time datalink transfer systems which link the aircraft with the Rivet Joint fleet. The datalinks are installed in Cobra Ball

for its theatre missile defence role to provide theatre commanders with real-time missile threat information.

A third RC-135S, 62-4128, entered service with the 45th RS in 1998 and is referred to as Cobra Ball II. Initially, the aircraft was not fully missionized and was not fitted with the full sensor suite but had an improved RTOS system installed.

By 2007, all three Cobra Ball aircraft were equipped with an upgraded fully missionized sensor suite, standard Rivet Joint communication links, and a high-bandwidth fibre-optic data distribution system. The Cobra Ball jets were the final RC-135 aircraft to receive the Pacer Crag glass cockpit and F108 engines.

LEFT • *A US Air Force RC-135S Cobra Ball aircraft assigned to the 45th Reconnaissance Squadron takes off from Offutt Air Force Base, Nebraska, May 8, 2019. The RC-135S Cobra Ball is a rapidly deployable aircraft, which flies joint chiefs of staff-directed missions of national priority to collect optical and electronic data on ballistic targets* US AIR FORCE PHOTO BY SENIOR AIRMAN JACOB SKOVO

Scientific and Technical Snooper

An overview of the RC-135U Combat Sent.

There are two RC-135s in operation with the 55th Wing which are non-Rivet Joint aircraft, both are designated as RC-135U and operate with the Combat Sent programme name. In comparison to the Rivet Joint, RC-135Us have a short nose radome, and are fitted with fairings in the chin, wingtips, tail cone, and fin-top which house the Precision Power Measurement System sensors, with a 360° coverage.

The primary mission objective for Combat Sent is to locate and identify foreign military land, naval, and airborne ELINT data, deemed to be the most interesting, the so-called scientific and technical ELINT. To enable the crew to detect and filter out the most interesting ELINT data several systems are fitted, which are believed to be unique to the RC-135U. These include a radar frequency measurement system, a spectrography and radiometer system, and thermal imaging. An extensive database holds all known emitter information, which allows non-interesting signals to be eliminated quickly.

Combat Sent aircraft are believed to be fitted with the expert mission manager (EMM), an automated system that provides fast ELINT collection of short transmission and 'hard-to-collect' signals emitted from supposedly 'secure' communication systems. EMM operates in real-time, validating, and re-identifying ELINT signals against several collected ELINT signal databases.

The EMM prioritises action against signals based on location, identifies the best location for the RC-135 to collect the signal, and recommends the systems to tune for the signal collection, ensuring that unknown signals are properly recorded for analysis. The objective is to automatically process all

RIGHT • *RC-135Us have a short nose radome, and are fitted with fairings in the chin, wingtips, tail cone, and fin-top which house the sensors for the Precision Power Measurement System, with a 360° coverage.* US AIR NATIONAL GUARD/SENIOR AIRMAN AMBER MULLEN

BELOW • *An RC-135U Combat Sent parked on the flightline at Wright Patterson Air Force Base in Dayton, Ohio.* US AIR NATIONAL GUARD/SENIOR AIRMAN AMBER MULLEN

known and usual signals away from the onboard intelligence officers, allowing them to concentrate on unknown and difficult signals.

Despite the 'smart' capability of the Combat Sent systems, some of the most modern emitters transmit signals on bandwidths and in wideband modulation that exceed the Combat Sent sensors ability to both receive and record the transmission.

Both RC-135Us are fitted with the Pacer Crag cockpit, high-resolution operator workstations with improved signal recognition, and a wide-band fibre-optic audio distribution network.

Air Sampling

An overview of the unique WC-135R Constant Phoenix.

Another unique role undertaken by the 55th Wing is the air-sampling mission using three WC-135R aircraft operated under the Constant Phoenix programme name. The Constant Phoenix aircraft were originally KC-135R aerial refuelling tanker aircraft. All missions flown by Constant Phoenix are treaty-derived missions to collect particulate and gaseous effluents and debris from accessible regions of the atmosphere in support of the Limited Nuclear Test Ban Treaty of 1963. The WC-135R is currently the only aircraft in the US inventory conducting air-sampling operations.

Constant Phoenix Systems

Constant Phoenix uses two sampling pods with U-1 foils fitted to the side of the upper fuselage aft of the main crew entrance door. Each sampling pod opens at both ends, albeit with no airflow leak, a pressure plate on the inside maintains the aircraft's pressurisation.

The air sampling filtration process is known as 'dragging the papers', a term derived from the filters used in the pods which are changed at a variety of intervals ranging from 30 minutes to two hours. Usually each filter is 'dragged' for more than two hours, the number of filters fitted varies according to the requirements of the mission but has gone up to eight.

Four compressors and four spheres equip the air-sampling system. Only three compressors run at any one time. The spheres collect and hold concentrated amounts of ambient air bled off from the engines, fed to the onboard compressors and compressed to 3,000psi. Much of the bled air is fed to a pneumatic system, which supplies the heating and pressurisation systems. The bleed air used for heating and pressurisation is passed through filters, colloquially known as lungs, the lungs protect the crew from any radioactive material that might be encountered during a mission. Any radioactive material particles are collected by cyndrical filters.

Operating Constant Phoenix

On a standard air-sampling mission the Constant Phoenix crew comprises two pilots, a navigator and two special equipment operators (SEOs). When the aircraft is forward deployed the crew is augmented by eight maintainers comprising a supervisor, two crew chiefs, and specialists in engines, hydraulics, electrical/environmental systems, communications/navigations systems, and guidance/control systems.

One SEO is required to operate the air-sampling system at the SEO position, which has instrumentation to provide positional awareness, sphere control and control of onboard detection instruments, which give an indication of what is being collected. The combined effect of the SEO instruments should place the aircraft in the correct position to conduct the mission requirements.

BELOW • *Maintainers receive WC-135R Constant Phoenix serial number 64-14831 for the first time at Offutt Air Force Base, Nebraska on May 11, 2023. Note the sampling pod fitted to the side of the upper fuselage.* US AIR FORCE/NICHOLAS HARNACK

ABOVE • *WC-135R Constant Phoenix tail number 64-14831 lands at Offutt Air Force Base, Nebraska on May 11, 2023.* US AIR FORCE/NICHOLAS HARNACK

The SEO instruments also provide advisory data for the crew exposure, for example by monitoring the levels of radiation. A second SEO takes care of changing filters and spheres and keeping an inventory of samples (where, when etc), tagging the samples and documenting each sample.

WC-135R Funding Details

FY2019 funding procured modification kits to convert three KC-135R aerial refuelling tanker aircraft to WC-135R Constant Phoenix configuration, and the required mission sensors for installation on the WC-135R aircraft.

The conversions were needed to address airframe viability concerns associated with the two aging WC-135Ws. Analysis determined that it was more cost-effective to convert KC-135R aircraft into WC-135s than to modify existing WC-135W aircraft to be on par with the rest of the C-135 variants (i.e., RC-135 and KC-135).

The first WC-135R, serial number 64-14836, arrived at Offutt on July 12, 2022, followed by 64-14831 on May 11, 2023. Aircraft 836 deployed to Muñiz Air Base, Puerto Rico, in January 2023, on the WC-135R's first overseas deployment.

The third and final WC-135R, serial number 64-14829, is scheduled to be delivered in the autumn of 2023.

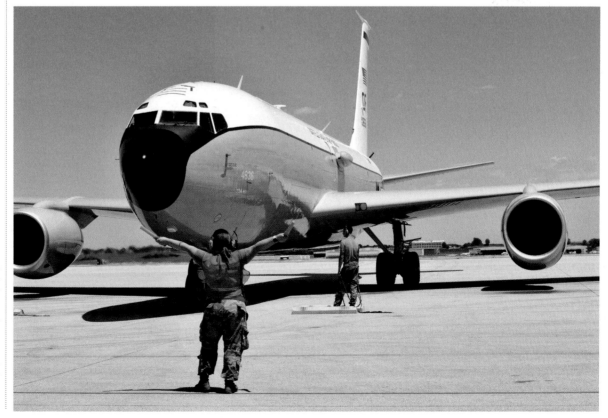

RIGHT • *WC-135R Constant Phoenix tail number 64-14836 taxies in after arriving at Lincoln Airport, Nebraska on July 11, 2022. Originally delivered to the US Air Force in 1964, the aircraft was modified into a WC-135R in Greenville, Texas, by the 645th Aeronautical Systems Group, better known as Big Safari.* US AIR FORCE/RYAN HANSEN

Recce Town

An overview of the Lockheed U-2 Dragon Lady high-altitude reconnaissance aircraft.

The 9th Reconnaissance Wing at Beale Air Force Base, California, known as Recce Town, is one of 12 units in the 16th Air Force that falls under Air Combat Command. The wing's mission is to deliver persistent, integrated reconnaissance to the nation, provided for the most part by the otherworldly U-2S Dragon Lady.

Operating at altitudes over 70,000ft, the U-2 is a reconnaissance aircraft that provides critical imagery to meet the intelligence needs of combatant commanders during any phase of peacetime or conflict.

Major Kelly, 9th Operations Support Squadron chief of wing weapons and tactics and a U-2 pilot explained the primary sensors: "ASARS, or the Advanced Synthetic Aperture Radar Sensor, uses radar energy to create an image of the target, making it an all-weather, day or night sensor. SYERS or Senior Year Electro-Optical Reconnaissance System is an electro-optical/infrared imaging sensor that takes images in the visible and infra-red spectrum to capture enhanced literal images. ASIP or Airborne Signals Intelligence Payload is the standard signals intelligence sensor that collects and analyses electronic signals emitted from a wide variety of targets.

"The U-2 employs at unmatched operational altitudes, which equates to unmatched sensor ranges from an airborne asset. This combination allows the U-2 to see further than any other airborne asset, and quickly adjust collection based on real-time circumstances."

The 9th Operations Group comprises the 1st and 99th Reconnaissance Squadrons, the 1st trains U-2 aircrew and the 99th conducts U-2 operations worldwide.

Kelly said the importance of ISR as a capability is twofold. "Before hostilities commence, ISR provides and updates the orders of battle that planners rely upon to understand the adversary and prepare for combat. Once combat operations begin, ISR is essential to finding, fixing, tracking, targeting, and assessing targets. ISR is the essential thread that finds, keeps custody of, and develops targets, and then judges how successfully the target was engaged."

Exercising Readiness

Between June 12-16, 2023, the 9th Reconnaissance Wing undertook Dragon Fang, a full-scale readiness exercise designed to test the wing's ability to rapidly deploy and perform mission essential tasks while in a mock deployed setting. The end goal of the exercise was to prepare the wing to transition to the new Air Force Force Generation deployment model.

BELOW • *U-2S Dragon Lady 80-1070/BB flies over the Golden Gate Bridge near San Francisco, California on a photo mission from Beale Air Force Base, about 130 miles to the northeast of the city.* US AIR FORCE/SSGT ROBERT TRUJILLO

RIGHT • *U-2S 80-1073 was originally a TR-1A but converted during February 1996. Seen at RAF Fairford in July 2017 returning to America after operations in the Middle East.* BOB ARCHER

Colonel Geoffrey Church, 9th Reconnaissance Wing commander said the purpose of the exercise was to test and evaluate the wing's ability to survive and operate during combat operations."

The week-long exercise involved 13 units assigned to the 9th RW, California Air National Guard's 195th Wing, and A Company of California Army National Guard's 140th Security and Support Aviation Battalion.

Technical Sergeant Channon Green, 9th RW wing inspection planner said: "The purpose of Dragon Fang is to evaluate and prepare us for the AFFORGEN model and to ensure that the 9th RW can give what is requested of them effectively, efficiently, and on time."

Airmen faced multiple tests of events that would lead up to a contested environment. Some of these events included airstrikes, ground assaults, chemical, biological, radiological, and nuclear events, and triage capabilities. Airmen were inspected on their ability to accomplish required mission essential tasks (METs) involving these scenarios."

Captain Miles Bliss, 9th RW director of inspections said: "An example of one of the METs we were testing was the ability to perform PAR [post attack reconnaissance] sweeps, so searching for UXO's [unexploded ordnance] post attack and making sure that the base was clear, doing recovery operations

BELOW • *U-2S 68-10336 spent much of its service conducting development work. During 2001 the aircraft was assigned to Warner Robins Air Logistics Center, at Robins Air Force Base, Georgia. For a limited period, the aircraft had the tail code 'LR' applied for Lockheed Robins.* BOB ARCHER COLLECTION

to check for damage to buildings and runways, and start repairs on them."

Members of the 9th Security Forces Squadron pulled airmen from different units to provide constant base defence while simultaneously being attacked and provided the first line of response to these events.

Captain Ricky Sizemore, 9th Security Forces Squadron operations officer said: "With this exercise, we implemented multi-capable airmen to fulfil force protection and security forces roles. This helps us build up a heightened defence posture and allows for more people to be in the fight."

The attacks resulted in injuries and casualties, but medical technicians

assigned to the 9th Medical Group quickly triaged patients based on the level of care needed, implemented Tactical Combat Catastrophe Care, and handled mortuary affairs.

Airmen from different agencies collaborated in the emergency operations centre to advise wing leadership on how to effectively employ the proper support needed to respond to the scenarios while still executing the mission.

Deployment Support
The 9th Logistics Readiness Squadron Individual Deployment Readiness Cell (IDRC) has an assigned team of airmen and civilians

ABOVE • *U-2S 80-1070/ BB flies above the Sierra Nevada Mountain Range, California. The aircraft is configured with a raft of antennas, an interchangeable nose and under wing slipper tanks housing advanced sensors, and an elliptical radome atop the centre fuselage housing Senior Span and Senior Spur satellite datalink systems.* US AIR FORCE/ SSGT ROBERT TRUJILLO

LEFT • *Pilots assigned to the 1st Reconnaissance Squadron prepare for take-off in a TU-2S aircraft at Beale Air Force Base, California on December 20, 2020.* US AIR FORCE/ SSGT RAMON ADELAN

comprising logistics planners, force support personnel, and an installation deployment officer that provides overall daily command and control for Beale's deployment process, and stands up as the Deployment Control Center (DCC) during large exercises or mass deployments.

Controlling movements, travel, supplies and making sure people get to their destination and back safely is a lengthy and daunting task. Explaining, a deployment operations officer said: "An effective deployment machine is mainly accomplished through a combined effort with unit deployment managers as we guide them throughout the process of pre-deployment preparation and ongoing maintenance of individual level readiness.

The deployment operations officer explained that Beale has a unique mission: "Our aircraft have a permanent presence in specific locations and our requirements are not swapped out with another wing at the end of a rotation, such as with fighters. This requires our personnel to maintain a high level of readiness year-round."

DCGS Distributed Surface Asset

Based at Beale Air Force Base, California, the 548th Intelligence, Surveillance, and Reconnaissance Group (ISRG) comprises four active-duty squadrons, two Air Force Reserve Command squadrons, two California Air National Guard squadrons, along with a geographically-separated detachment at Davis-Monthan Air Force Base, Arizona.

The 9th Intelligence Squadron (IS) conducts analysis and processing, exploitation, and dissemination (PED) functions for MQ-9 collection and is the US Air Force's only unit processing and exploiting U-2 Optical Bar Camera imagery.

The 13th IS conducts PED operations for high-altitude (U-2 and RQ-4) signals and imagery intelligence collection.

RIGHT • *Approaching 53 years of service, U-2S 68-10337 seen at RAF Mildenhall in August 2020, in the latest configuration. The aircraft achieved 20,000 flight hours on September 20, 2000, while deployed to the Middle East. This despite an accident in Thailand in May 1975, and another at Patrick Air Force Base, Florida in May 1988.* BOB ARCHER

The 48th IS provides maintenance and sustainment to segments of the Distributed Common Ground System (DCGS) weapon system.

In 2021, the 548th ISRG commissioned a new DCGS called a DCGS Distributed Surface Asset (DDSA) which replaced the Modularized Interoperable Surface Terminal (MIST).

Explaining the DDSA, Lieutenant Denny Yang, assigned to the 48th IS said: "The DDSA sends out radio waves that are picked up by a transmitter receiver on the U-2 allowing for the two systems to communicate."

According to Kenneth Lier, the 48th IS deputy director of operations: "The plane takes the image or collects the data, and then operators can download it quickly to be exploited. Operators do that through the tether

via satellite, or within the radius of the DDSA.

"Beale is unique in that its aircraft platforms are co-located with a DCGS. This allows a greater level of cooperation between the intelligence mission and the flying mission. It helps pilots train with data link operations before flying real-world missions.

"Satellite time is very expensive. The 9th RW doesn't want to buy satellite time to train pilots, so we use our [tether] for pilot training. It's a lot cheaper and it's easier to coordinate. Not only does the DDSA allow for easier pilot training, but it also expedites the testing of sensors before aircraft are deployed.

"Before the wing sends a sensor overseas to a location where the wing is operating, the wing wants to make sure the sensor is good. That's another

capability that they utilise by having the colocation of the U-2 and DDSA. We can pre-check the sensors and make sure they're functional before they are deployed."

U-2 Crew Chiefs

The 9th Aircraft Maintenance Squadron and its expeditionary counterparts' crew chiefs are responsible for launching every U-2 Dragon Lady sortie across the globe.

Based at Sheppard Air Force Base, Texas, the 372nd Training Squadron trains crew chiefs for most US Air Force types. The squadron's Detachment 21 is based at Beale Air Force Base and is the only mission ready airman technical school for U-2s in the US Air Force. Students arrive at Det 21 from Sheppard to learn the core tasks of how to work on, modify and fix a U-2 over 45 days of instruction with three to six students per class and 30 per year.

Instruction includes the hydrazine system, engines, electronics, fuels, flight controls, and hands on experience with launching and recovering, servicing nitrogen, and performing inspections.

Over the 45-day course, students complete two blocks of instruction. The first block comprises all classroom instruction where students learn how components relate and work together to make the U-2 aircraft fly. Block two comprises all flightline tasks: refuelling and defueling an aircraft, marshalling an aircraft, parking, launching an aircraft, and operating technical orders which contains the information and details required to operate the jet.

Phase Maintenance

Ensuring the long-term performance of the U-2 falls upon a team of airmen in the 9th Maintenance Squadron who perform phase maintenance on the airframe. Phase maintenance is a periodic inspection of the aircraft undertaken every 1,000 flying hours. The process involves breaking the aircraft down by removing panels, inspecting the aircraft for broken parts,

changing out parts that are due for replacement, reassembling the aircraft and testing it.

According to Technical Sergeant Garrett Jensen, a phase dock chief assigned to the 9th Maintenance Squadron the 1,000-hour phase inspection process takes approximately 12 days to complete while a minor phase, which occurs every 500 flying hours, takes seven days.

Senior Airman Jonathan Blaker, a repair and reclamation specialist assigned to the 9th Maintenance Squadron said: "Our main priority is the rudder, elevator and aileron cables. Over time cables will wear out and the metal wears down. When we find something wrong, we replace it and string a new cable along the whole aircraft. Each of the canopies is also uniquely fitted to the jet. We must shave it, trim it, and bend it to form it to the cockpit."

Phase maintenance on the U-2 can often be back-to-back and sometimes overlaps due to a unique programme in which the 9th Maintenance Squadron serves as the maintenance hub with responsibility for maintaining jets in operational and expeditionary locations.

TSgt Jensen said: "Under the global phase programme we are responsible for doing phase on the entire fleet. When aircraft in Korea are due for phase maintenance, we send a team of four to six people out there. Members of the phase shop regularly go TDY to

ABOVE • *A pilot steers a U-2S to its parking spot while being marshalled by a crew chief. The aircraft is assigned to the 99th Expeditionary Reconnaissance Squadron at Al Dhafra Air Base, United Arab Emirates.* US AIR FORCE/ MSGT JENIFER CALHOUN

LEFT • *Major William Gottenberg, a U-2 pilot with the 99th Expeditionary Reconnaissance Squadron, steers U-2S 80-1087/BB to a parking spot after completing his 100th combat mission in the U-2.* US AIR FORCE/MSGT JENIFER CALHOUN

BELOW • *A U-2 pilot drives a high-performance chase car down the runway to catch a U-2 performing a low touch and go at Al Dhafra Air Base, United Arab Emirates. The pilot driving the chase car helps the pilot flying the U-2 by communicating alignment with and height above the runway during take-offs and landings.* US AIR FORCE/ SENIOR AIRMAN GRACIE LEE

RIGHT • *A U-2 pilot assigned to the 99th Expeditionary Reconnaissance Squadron, taxiess a U-2 Dragon Lady .* US AIR FORCE/MSGT JENNIFER CALHOUN

Osan Air Base, Republic of Korea, RAF Fairford, England, and Joint Base Pearl Harbor-Hickam, Hawaii.

"Our work is meticulous, and it requires attention to detail and research, but it is important we do it right. We deliver quality aircraft back out to the flightline so they can have another 1,000 flying hours."

Propulsion Shop

The U-2's GE Aviation F118-GE-101 engine is maintained at the 9th RW by the 9th Maintenance Squadron aerospace propulsion shop with responsibility for the flightline maintenance, ensuring serviceability after every flight,

RIGHT • *A U-2 Dragon Lady taxies to its parking spot at Al Dhafra Air Base in the United Arab Emirates.* US AIR FORCE/MSGT JENNIFER CALHOUN

conducting oil analysis, and any time-based maintenance.

Master Sergeant Byron Johnson, a flight chief with the 9th MXS said: "Working on the U-2 engine is unique. Unlike other aircraft that allow for relatively easy access to the engine, we have to disassemble it and pull off the entire back half of the aircraft. Changing filters and constantly looking the engine over keep it running smoothly. We find small things occasionally, that if neglected could lead to bigger problems later. Sometimes if the engine doesn't come out for a little while a small problem could manifest itself into something bigger, so it is important we address it right away."

Fuel Systems

Maintenance of the U-2's fuel components is the responsibility of the 9th Maintenance Squadron's aircraft fuel systems.

"When the aircraft come down and the crew chiefs see a fuel leak or issue with one of our components, they'll call us out to evaluate the leak or troubleshoot the issue. Knowing the aircraft and how our parts work allows us to troubleshoot different possibilities and narrow it down to the exact problem. For instance,

RIGHT • *U-2 aircraft were deployed to Al Dhafra Air Base, United Arab Emirates from Beale Air Force Base, California, and assigned to the 380th Air Expeditionary Wing.* US AIR FORCE/MSGT JENNIFER CALHOUN

BELOW • *Over the last 20 years, U-2s deployed to Al Dhafra Air Base, United Arab Emirates supported Operations Iraqi Freedom and Enduring Freedom and the Combined Joint Task Force-Horn of Africa.* US AIR FORCE/MSGT JENNIFER CALHOUN

a boost pump's pressure read out is supposed to be 10 to 20 PSI," said Senior Airman Steven Benton, a fuels systems technician with the 9th MXS.

One important task for the aircraft fuel systems shop is maintaining the hydrazine and emergency start system. Explaining, Staff Sergeant Kirk Smith, 9th Maintenance Squadron aircraft fuel systems craftsman said: "The emergency start system is a one-time chance to restart the engine if something goes wrong during flight. To work on it, we must be certified to work with hydrazine."

Aircrew Flight Equipment

Specialists assigned to the aircrew flight equipment shop of the 9th Operations Support Squadron are responsible for ensuring pilots' equipment is up to date and safe for use.

"We inspect and maintain their gear regularly to ensure all their equipment is in perfect working condition," said Airman 1st Class Joshua Chatman.

When inspecting or maintaining equipment, a pilot's safety is the number one priority, and for that reason aircrew flight equipment specialists use the Defense Property Accountability System (DPAS). Details of all inspections and maintenance conducted on flight equipment are input to the system, with a weekly run through of the flight's overdue list to make sure nothing has been missed.

LEFT • *An airman shuts off a liquid oxygen container after refilling the liquid oxygen system of a U-2 Dragon Lady.*

BELOW • *A U-2 Dragon Lady at Al Dhafra Air Base, United Arab Emirates.*

ABOVE • *A U-2 Dragon Lady taxies from the flightline at Beale Air Force Base, California.* US AIR FORCE/ AIRMAN JULIANA LONDONO

RIGHT • *A U-2 Dragon Lady lands at Beale Air Force Base, California following a surveillance and reconnaissance mission of the Gulf Coast region from Lake Charles, Louisiana to Brownsville, Texas in preparation of Hurricane Rita, requested by the Federal Emergency Management Agency.* US AIR FORCE

Oxygen masks, oxygen tanks, parachutes, g-suits, helmets, and survival kits are just a portion of the variety of equipment maintained by the aircrew flight equipment shop.

Egress Systems

Ejection is a pilot's last chance at survival. Their lives rest in the hands of aircrew egress system specialists assigned to 9th Maintenance Squadron who inspect, maintain and service all aircraft egress systems installed on U-2,

TU-2 and T-38 aircraft assigned to the 9th RW to ensure they are functioning properly.

Discussing the work, Staff Sergeant Cody Clark, 9th Maintenance Squadron aircrew egress craftsman said: "We try to schedule anywhere from two to three seats in a typical week, and that's not including unscheduled maintenance that could pop up. The work has no margin for error. Airmen at the egress shop rely on each other to make sure the job gets done. But I feel confident knowing that our crew

executed everything perfectly because we do not settle for anything less than perfection."

Petroleum, Oil and Lubricants

Liquid Oxygen (LOX) called Aviator's Breathing Oxygen (ABO) is a pilot's main source of air at altitudes exceeding 10,000 feet - it's paramount to U-2 pilots and the mission.

In the 9th RW, LOX is provided by airmen assigned to the 9th Logistics Readiness Squadron

(LRS) fuels cryogenics technicians working for the Petroleum, Oil and Lubricants Airmen (POL).

Fuels cryogenics technicians don white personal protective equipment to ensure airmen are safe while handling LOX and performing tests.

Airman 1st Class Randy Willis, a 9th LRS cryogenics technician said: "We wear specialised protective gear to prevent our skin from burns because the LOX is pressurised gas at minus 297° Fahrenheit. After servicing and testing, the LOX is delivered to and put into the aircraft for the pilots to use."

Aerospace Ground Equipment

To support U-2 maintenance and flying operations at Beale, the 9th Maintenance Squadron aerospace ground equipment (AGE) flight inspects, maintains, modifies, and repairs all aerospace ground equipment that supplies electricity, hydraulic pressure, and air pressure to the wing's assigned aircraft.

The AGE flight which is responsible for over 500 pieces of equipment is divided into four different sections: maintenance performs major fixes, inspection does preventative maintenance and minor fixes, service and delivery deliver the equipment to the requesting units, and

support provides the tools needed to fix equipment.

TR-1 and U-2S

Twenty years after Gary Powers made world headline news when his aircraft was shot down over central Russia, the name U-2 was still synonymous with everything bad about intelligence gathering. Consequently, when the US Air Force wished to re-open the

production line to construct a version dedicated to battlefield surveillance in Europe, senior personnel considered it prudent to allocate an alternative designation.

Lockheed understood that it was sensible to build new aircraft for the task rather than develop unmanned aerial vehicles. An order was placed for 37 aircraft in November 1979, using existing jigs and tooling, but constructed

ABOVE • *A U-2 Dragon Lady lands at Al Dhafra Air Base, United Arab Emirates, an operational detachment location deployed from Beale Air Force Base, California.* US AIR NATIONAL GUARD/ SSGT COLTON ELLIOTT

LEFT • *A U-2 Dragon Lady landing at Al Dhafra Air Base, United Arab Emirates.* US AIR NATIONAL GUARD/SSGT COLTON ELLIOTT

RIGHT • *Physiology technicians help a U-2 Dragon Lady pilot into his full pressure suit.* US AIR FORCE/SENIOR AIRMAN GRACIE LEE

RIGHT • *Commonly referred to as the most difficult aircraft to fly in the world, the U-2 Dragon Lady has been flown by less than 1,500 pilots since the first flight in 1955.* US AIR FORCE/SENIOR AIRMAN GRACIE LEE

BELOW • *A U-2 Dragon Lady assigned to the 99th Expeditionary Reconnaissance Squadron prepares for a mission in support of Operation Inherent Resolve from Al Dhafra Air Base, United Arab Emirates.* US AIR FORCE/SENIOR AIRMAN GRACIE LEE

at Palmdale, California. The majority were to become the TR-1, although some retained the U-2 designation despite an identical external appearance.

First to roll-out from the Palmdale line was TR-1A 80-1066 on July 15, 1981, with delivery to Beale Air Force Base in September.

Eight were designated U-2Rs, one a U-2R(T) dedicated to training, two as ER-2s for the National Aeronautics and Space Administration, two TR-1B trainer versions and the remaining 24 as operational TR-1A versions.

TR-1A 80-1068 was the first to visit Europe, arriving on August 30, 1982, for display at the Farnborough Air Show. It was hoped to generate export orders, possibly including the UK and Germany, although no further interest was forthcoming.

Earlier, the decision had been made to station TR-1s at RAF Alconbury, England where the 17th Reconnaissance Wing and its flying component, the 95th Reconnaissance Squadron, both activated on October 1, 1982. The wing was accountable to SAC's 7th Air Division, with headquarters at Ramstein Air Base, West Germany, who organised day-to-day tasking on behalf of United States Air Forces in Europe.

The first pair of TR-1As, 80-1068 and 80-1070, was delivered to Alconbury during February 1983, and because the TR-1 was capable of assuming the intelligence gathering duties and its own battlefield tasking, the U-2R assigned to Detachment 4 at RAF Mildenhall ceased operations. Consequently, the final resident U-2R, 68-10337 returned to Beale Air Force Base.

RAF Mildenhall's association with the U-2 began in June 1977 on the basis of short-term visits but changed to a full-time basis on March 30, 1979, when 68-10338 arrived.

TR-1A deliveries to Alconbury were slow, largely because the aircraft's dedicated sensors were being developed at a somewhat leisurely pace. Missions were quite often flown to West Germany

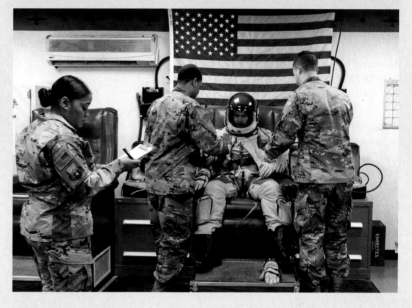

and the Baltic Sea area, to monitor the traditional Warsaw Pact nations, with sorties lasting up to nine hours.

Thirteen huge, hardened aircraft shelters were constructed by 1989, with roughly that number of aircraft assigned. As new sensors including the Precision Location Strike System and the ASAR-2 were developed, aircraft were either retrofitted at Alconbury, or during Program Depot Maintenance at the Warner Robins Air Logistics Center in Georgia.

The end of the Cold War largely negated the presence of a TR-1 force in Europe. Consequently, the Alconbury-based 95th Reconnaissance Squadron became a direct reporting unit to the 9th Strategic Reconnaissance Wing and the 17th Reconnaissance Wing was inactivated on June 30, 1991. Its assigned aircraft began to depart in August 1991. Half the fleet had left the Cambridgeshire base by the year end.

In October 1991, all the surviving TR-1As were re-designated as U-2R aircraft.

The deteriorating situation in the Balkans required regular monitoring, with the 95th Reconnaissance Squadron supporting a temporary assignment of a Beale based U-2 equipped with the Senior Span system at Naval Air Station Sigonella, Sicily in April 1992. Later that year, the same jet deployed to Aviano Air Base, Italy. However, neither facility was ideally suited for supporting missions over the Balkans so subsequent sorties were flown from Alconbury.

The 95th Reconnaissance Squadron was inactivated on September 15, 1993, with its subsequent activities falling under Operating Location-United Kingdom (OL-UK). This enabled sorties to be undertaken with temporary duty personnel. RAF Alconbury was reduced to reserve base status, and on March 15, 1995, the remaining three aircraft relocated to RAF Fairford, the new temporary home for OL-UK. To this day, the Gloucestershire base continues to host U-2 operations, and supports transit flights between the United States, RAF Akrotiri, Cyprus, and the Middle East.

Current Situation

Pratt & Whitney's J75 engine had powered the U-2 since its earliest days, but developments in design enabled the more powerful and lighter General Electric F118-GE-F29 to be installed for the first time in May 1989. This was a difficult integration. Protracted trials and delayed funding prevented F118 engines from entering service until October 1994 with the aircraft then designated as the U-2S and TU-2S. Thirty-seven aircraft received F118 engines; both NASA ER-2s, all four TU-2S trainer and 31 U-2S aircraft.

The U-2S remains the US Air Force's only manned, strategic, high-altitude, long range ISR platform, capable of signals intelligence (SIGINT), imagery intelligence (IMINT) - the new name for photography, and measurement and signature intelligence (MASINT) collection.

Intelligence gathering requires sensors and the U-2S can carry some of the most advanced devices ever produced. These can be installed in a variety of interchangeable noses, and within slipper tanks, positioned on both wings. These can carry a wide variety of advanced optical, multispectral, synthetic aperture radar, SIGINT, and other payloads simultaneously.

Sensor bays permit rapid installation of new equipment to counter emerging threats and requirements.

ABOVE • *U-2 pilot prepares to enter the cockpit of a U-2 Dragon Lady as a launch and recovery technician prepares to assist with the hook up.* US AIR FORCE/AIRMAN 1ST CLASS DREW BUCHANAN

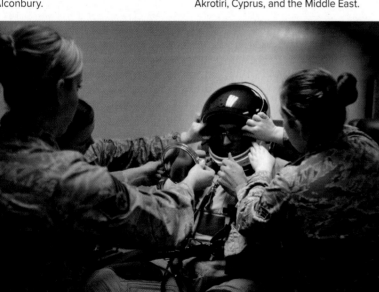

LEFT • *A launch and recovery technician uses a mirror to confirm placement of the pilot's specialised glasses within his helmet. Donning of the highly specialised full pressure suit requires a team of physiological support personnel.* US AIR FORCE/AIRMAN 1ST CLASS DREW BUCHANAN

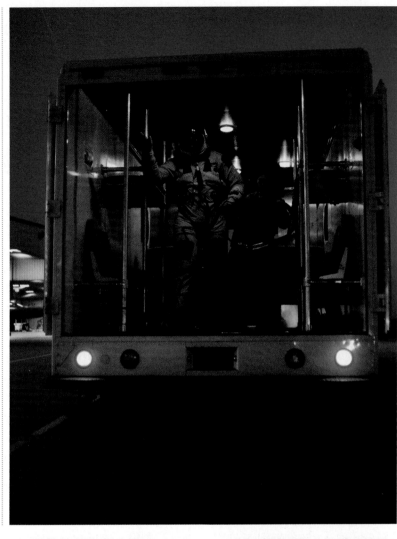

RIGHT • *A U-2 pilot prepares to exit a physiological support vehicle on the flightline at Beale Air Force Base, California prior to a mission.* US AIR FORCE/ AIRMAN 1ST CLASS DREW BUCHANAN

BELOW • *Maintenance personnel from the 9th Aircraft Maintenance Squadron stand by as the pilot and a launch and recovery technician prepare the cockpit of a U-2 at Beale Air Force Base, California.* US AIR FORCE/AIRMAN 1ST CLASS DREW BUCHANAN

U-2s comprise 50% of the high-altitude ISR fleet and are heavily tasked. Recent improvements to Block 20 configuration, feature a glass cockpit, digital autopilot, modernised electronic warfare system, and updated data links.

Major sensors are Raytheon's ASAR-2A advanced synthetic aperture radar system, the UTC Aerospace SYERS-2A Senior Year electro-optical imagery system, and the enhanced ASIP airborne signals intelligence payload. Data gathered is linked via satellite by the Senior Span and Senior Spur systems housed in a large elliptical radome atop the centre fuselage to ground stations for exploitation. The legacy optical bar camera system is also still used to provide broad-area imagery.

The fleet is currently undergoing upgrades to Block 20.1 standard, adding ASAR-2B, next-generation SIGINT, avionics and navigation improvements, and modernisation of the Link-16 datalink and the multi-function advanced datalink.

ASAR-2B significantly improves the U-2 deep-look radar's ground mapping, moving target, and maritime modes. Two ASAR-2B-equipped aircraft began flight testing in FY2022, with initial operational capability expected in FY2023.

U-2S aircraft are also receiving stellar and GPS navigation, quick-

aerial vehicles and satellites can
perform most of the aircraft's mission
functions. However, on each occasion
the U-2 proved to be more capable,
and far more flexible than satellite and
unmanned aerial systems.

Under present arrangements, the
U-2 has a guaranteed service life until
at least 2025, but Lockheed Martin
claims the airframes could fly until at
least 2050.

Beale Air Force Base in northern
California is home to the 9th
Reconnaissance Wing and its
component U-2 squadrons: the
1st Reconnaissance Squadron as
the formal training unit, and the
99th Reconnaissance Squadron as
the operational squadron. The 1st
Reconnaissance Squadron flies the
TU-2S two-seat trainer, the U-2S and
the T-38C Talon as a proficiency trainer.

Overseas the 5th Reconnaissance
Squadron at Osan Air Base, Republic of
Korea monitors activities on the Korean
peninsula, China, and eastern Russia.
At RAF Akrotiri, Cyprus, Detachment
1 monitors North Africa and eastern
Mediterranean nations, while the
99th Expeditionary Reconnaissance
Squadron at Al Dhafra Air Base in the
UAE provides ISR missions across
the Middle East and southwest Asia
and retains operational responsibility

ABOVE • *Maintainers
from the 9th Aircraft
Maintenance Squadron
salute the pilot as he
prepares for a mission.*
US AIR FORCE/AIRMAN 1ST
CLASS DREW BUCHANAN

LEFT • *The pilot checks
his heads-up display
in the cockpit of a U-2
Dragon Lady. The current
U-2S model features an
all-glass, digital cockpit,
improved sensors, and
propulsion system.* US AIR
FORCE/AIRMAN 1ST CLASS
DREW BUCHANAN

change modular mission systems,
and upgrades of multispectral sensor
and electronic warfare systems.
Airframe modifications, refreshing of
helmet and pressure suits, and egress
improvements are also ongoing.

A host of contractors sustain the
U-2. Lockheed Martin supports the
airframes and much of the systems
integration, while the following
companies support and continue
to enhance their sensor systems:
Northrop Grumman (ASIP), Raytheon
(ASAR), and UTC Aerospace (SYERS/
Optical Bar Camera).

At the time of writing, the US Air
Force claims its inventory to comprise
27 U-2S and four TU-2S aircraft, which
would seem correct. One TR-1A/U-2R
was subsequently converted to a TU-2S
and was lost, as were two more U-2S
aircraft. Another U-2S remains on long-
term rebuild at Palmdale, following a
serious fire at Al Dhafra Air Base, in the
United Arab Emirates.

Painted in a matt black paint scheme,
the sinister-looking U-2 has been the
subject of several attempts by various
government organisations to retire
the type, usually citing that unmanned

for U-2S operations at RAF Fairford, England.

Ongoing test and evaluation are performed by Det 2, 563rd Test and Evaluation Group at Beale, but uses aircraft from the host wing.

Air Force Materiel Command's Warner Robins Air Logistics Complex at Robins Air Force Base, Georgia, occasionally uses a U-2S for development work. The ALC also performs some Program Depot maintenance and manages the work to be completed by Lockheed Martin at its Palmdale facility.

In its seventh decade of operation, the U-2 is more effective today than when missions first began. What's more, there is every chance the U-2 will continue for another 20 years, which would continue its operation to nine decades - a truly remarkable achievement.

U-2S Tech Refresh

In September 2023, Lockheed Martin Skunk Works, in partnership with the US Air Force, completed the first flight of the U-2 Dragon Lady's Avionics Tech Refresh (ATR) programme. The first flight involved a low-altitude functional check flight to integrate new avionics, cabling, and software as part of the ATR contract, including:

• An updated avionics suite (communications, navigation, display, etc.) that modernises the U-2's onboard systems to readily accept and use new technology.

• A new mission computer designed to the US Air Force's open mission systems (OMS) standard that enables the U-2 to integrate with systems across air, space, sea, land, and cyber domains at disparate security levels.

• New modern cockpit displays to make pilot tasks easier, while enhancing presentation of the data the aircraft collects to enable faster, better-informed decisions.

The ATR first flight marked a milestone in the U-2's modernisation efforts and its path to be the first fully Open Mission System-compliant fleet. Further testing will solidify a mature software baseline before mission systems are introduced to ensure both functionality and interoperability to meet operational needs.

The U-2 ATR contract valued at $50m was awarded by the US Air Force in 2020.

Agile Combat Employment with a U-2

Mark Ayton provides an account of the first evolution agile combat employment with the U-2.

On March 25, 2023, a single U-2S Dragon Lady and airmen assigned to the 9th Reconnaissance Wing based at Beale Air Force Base, California, deployed to Offutt Air Force Base, Nebraska for Exercise Dragon Flag East.

The exercise was staged to further prepare the 9th RW for potential Agile Combat Employment (ACE) operations around the world to meet combatant commanders' objectives and in accordance with the United States' National Defense Strategy.

During Dragon Flag East, airmen executed collaborative reconnaissance missions using the U-2S and RC-135 Rivet Joint aircraft based at Offutt to provide adaptable, agile combat support to the combatant command. This involved working with the 55th Wing's multi-capable airmen (MCA) cell to advance cross-utilisation of their core career specialties.

Colonel Kristen Thompson, 55th Wing commander said: "The effort is designed to improve how we collect, analyse, and share information and make operational decisions more effectively than our potential adversaries and increases our survivability in a contested environment."

Exercise participants were drawn from numerous squadrons from the 9th RW and the 55th Wing.

The exercise, staged between March 27 and April 7, 2023 created an opportunity for the 9th RW to reposition and join forces with the 55th Wing at Offutt, and simulate combat operational challenges experienced overseas.

ABOVE • *A fuels facilities technician assigned to the 55th Logistics Readiness Squadron assists 9th LRS personnel to fuel the U-2 Dragon Lady at Offutt Air Force Base, Nebraska, on March 29, 2023.*
US AIR FORCE/LT HAILEY MALAY

Agile Combat Employment

The ACE concept requires a squadron to deploy a bare minimum of equipment and personnel to a location that's unfamiliar and conduct flight operations. A multi-capable airman can work in more than one Air Force Speciality Code, for example, an avionics specialist fuelling an aircraft, a task usually done by a crew chief. Consequently, multi-capable

airman support ACE by minimising manpower while maintaining operations.

As the exercise progressed airmen assigned to both wings employed lead wing concepts while simultaneously conducting collaborative intelligence, surveillance. and reconnaissance operations to meet the combatant commander's objectives: the 55th Wing was the lead wing.

The two wings designed and executed Exercise Dragon Flag East to simulate ACE from non-standard operating locations for the U-2 Dragon Lady. The exercise involved integration of the U-2 and RC-135 Rivet Joint weapon systems for future collaborative ISR operations in support of the National Defense Strategy.

Col Thompson said: "As a lead wing, we must be prepared to

LEFT • *An electrical and environmental systems craftsman assigned to the 9th Aircraft Maintenance Squadron supplies liquid oxygen to a U-2 Dragon Lady during Dragon Flag East at Offutt Air Force Base, Nebraska. Liquid oxygen is converted into a gaseous state for pilots to breathe during flight, allowing for long duration, high-altitude sorties.* US AIR FORCE/ AIRMAN 1ST CLASS JULIANA LONDONO

RIGHT • *A crew chief assigned to the 9th Aircraft Maintenance Squadron fuels a U-2 Dragon Lady during Exercise Dragon Flag East. The fuelling process undertaken by airmen assigned to both the 9th Reconnaissance Wing and the 55th Wing took approximately 45 minutes to complete.* US AIR FORCE/AIRMAN 1ST CLASS JULIANA LONDONO

BELOW • *A US Air Force 9th Aircraft Maintenance Squadron crew chief assesses a U-2 Dragon Lady after fuelling during Exercise Dragon Flag East. In support of the exercise, Agile Combat Employment manoeuvres were used in moving the U-2's thermally stable fuel.* US AIR FORCE/AIRMAN 1ST CLASS JULIANA LONDONO

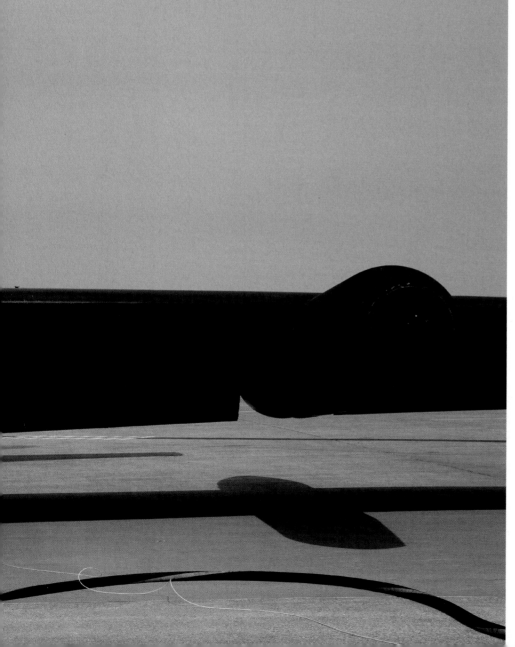

provide command and control to any platform the air force has. Dragon Flag East was an opportunity to train directly with the 9th RW and further develop our tactics and cross-flow of intelligence gathering capabilities."

The RC-135 provides near real-time on-scene intelligence collection, analysis, and dissemination capabilities, while the U-2 provides all-weather, high-resonance imagery and signals intelligence while flying at altitudes above 70,000ft.

Practising the ACE concept enabled both wings to determine the size of each team and support equipment needed to execute the mission.

A 9th Logistics Readiness Squadron NCO in charge of deployment planning said: "We took the U-2 package, we slimmed it down to make sure we had a very small footprint, we didn't disrupt the base whatsoever, we completed our mission and had a quick turnaround of getting back home. It shows that we can go anywhere, anytime with the least amount of things and still get our job done."

A team of four airmen assigned to the 9th Physiological Support Squadron overcame various challenges and executed the mission. A section chief said: "We're the launch and recovery teams, so we integrate the pilot with the suit, then we integrate the pilot and suit, into the jet. ACE is important if we enter conflict with a peer adversary, some locations will become unusable at some point. So, proving that we can function at locations without

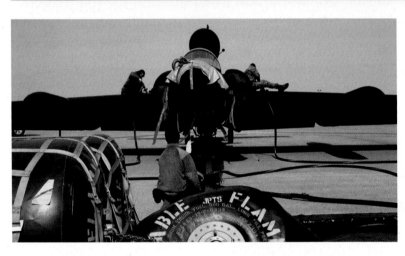

The lead wing team arrived at a site void of communications capabilities and facilities on the first day. Working with civil engineers assigned to Nebraska Air National Guard's 155th Air Refueling Wing and airmen assigned to the 52nd Combat Communications Squadron based at Warner Robins Air Force Base, Georgia, the group erected two tents with redundant satellite connections to the air force radio and computer networks at multiple security levels.

prior preparation is a useful set of data to have."

Two intelligence analysts assigned to the 9th Operational Support Squadron provided intelligence analysis and imagery dissemination to key decision makers during Dragon Flag East. One analyst said: "We've learned how the Rivet Joint crew - their pilots, navigation planners, and intel analysts - operates, and we were able to closely integrate throughout the exercise and sustained the U-2 mission with just two of us."

Colonel Geoffrey Church, 9th RW commander said: "We are always postured to continue sustaining and assessing mission readiness, especially ACE and MCA concepts. Dragon Flag East was the culmination of our ongoing efforts to build resilient, ready warfighters."

Iron Recce

During Exercise Dragon Flag East, the 55th Wing conducted a three-day lead wing exercise to test its ability to conduct command and control along with mission generation force element integration in a contested environment through simulated competition-through-conflict actions against a peer competitor.

Colonel Mark Howard, 55th Wing vice commander and exercise lead wing deputy commander said: "To prepare for lead wing responsibilities, we developed an internal exercise called Iron Recce. As a newly designated lead wing, we need to demonstrate our ability to command and control air force assets from multiple locations.

"Our scenario complicated adversary targeting by locating our wing operations centre at one base, then our F-16 fighters from the [Alabama Air National Guard's] 187th Fighter Wing and our intelligence, surveillance, reconnaissance and airborne electronic attack assets from the Fightin' 55th at different locations."

The two facilities housed a robust communications node, enabling the A-Staff to command-and-control multiple mission generation force elements, one housed a Wing Operations Center (WOC), the other housed a Temporary Sensitive Compartmented Information Facility (T-SCIF).

The following day, lead wing staff worked through a variety of scenarios that tested their ability to operate from the facilities using the communications equipment set up.

Explaining the facilities, Col Howard said: "We had several layers of connectivity - top-secret internet and phone capability, secret text messaging, along with encrypted and secure radios. We were communicating with a simulated Air Operations Center Node located at Offutt Air Force Base and using the exercise injects to drive our decision making as a team. Several times during the exercise, we simulated losing connectivity with the AOC at critical points to force

us to meet the commander's intent without having specific directions from higher headquarters. In our Wing Operations Center tent, my A-Staff would advise me on how the scenario injects impacted operations and we had to make timely decisions to ensure mission accomplishment."

On the third and final day of Exercise Iron Recce, the team tested its ability to move the equipment and re-establish the WOC and T-SCIF in the event of an impending attack at their initial location.

Sneaky King Airs

David Isby reviews the RC-12X Guardrail, MC-12S EMARSS and other US Army ISR platforms.

In 1946, during the opening months of the Cold War, both US and British forces had to improvise twin-engine signals intelligence (SIGINT) aircraft. Flying up the air corridors to Berlin, Project Bourbon pioneered coalition airborne intelligence, surveillance and (ISR) efforts. This continued for decades, integrating both country's SIGINT and communications intelligent (COMINT) efforts with visual and photographic intelligence. Eventually the project included the use of enhanced electro-optical and infrared (EO/IR) technologies, to provide confirmation as to the type and location of the source of electronic emissions.

Today, a new generation of US and British SIGINT-capable twin-engine, medium-altitude ISR aircraft carry out similar missions. They provide invaluable information for a reasonable operating cost. Many other air arms with limited force structure and resources, that do not need (and cannot afford) the few high-end four-engine ISR platforms such as those operated by the US and Britain, make effective use of twin-engine aircraft with integrated sensor suites allowing a single aircraft to be equipped with SIGINT, COMINT and multi-spectral sensor capabilities.

LEFT • *An MC-12W Liberty pilot assigned to the 185th Special Operations Squadron, conducts pre-flight checks at Joint Base San Antonio-Lackland, Texas.* US AIR FORCE/ MATTHEW MCGOVERN

Today's aircraft are a far cry from their improvised predecessors, but still benefit from the lessons of how they were deployed and used in the past.

Twin Engine Multi-Spectral ISR

Decades later, the need for improvisation to enable SIGINT capability as part of an effective airborne ISR capability became apparent during the conflicts in Afghanistan and Iraq.

Insurgents made effective use of tactical radios and cell phones to both communicate and trigger improvised

explosive devices (IEDs). The US Air Force, the US Army, the Royal Air Force, and other coalition partners with deployed troops, found these threats a challenge to counter. The limited number of specialised aircraft capable of ISR missions – especially SIGINT – were already committed to combat and were flying to high operational tempos. Sensors on those aircraft – whether a suite integrated on large multi-engine jets or a pod-mounted system on tactical aircraft – were not intended for the counterinsurgency role. Suitable ISR aircraft optimised for the role were urgently needed.

BELOW • *RC-12D 81-23542 at RAF Mildenhall, England on September 30, 1984, during a refuelling stop on its delivery flight to the 1st Military Intelligence Battalion at Wiesbaden, West Germany.* BOB ARCHER

The US Army had used multiple versions of twin-engine Beechcraft types configured for the SIGINT mission, the earliest RU-8 Seminoles date back to the 1950s.

US Army RC-12 Guard Rail aircraft were used from the opening stages of the conflicts in Afghanistan and Iraq. But their sensor suites were not designed to deal with cell phones (see later). Additionally, the RC-12s still had other worldwide commitments, so the Army supplemented them with Beechcraft King Air 350ER twin turboprops. The 350ERs were fitted with an integrated sensor suite developed by the Sierra Nevada Corporation. Named the Enhanced Medium Altitude Reconnaissance and Surveillance System or EMARRS, it provides the US Army with a specialised sensor platform that effectively supplements high-end ISR aircraft.

The multi-spectral system featured radar, EO/IR, SIGINT, Ku-band SATCOM, and the tactical common data link. As one of many sensor suites in use across the battlespace, MARSS was vital for distinguishing local people from potential insurgent targets.

Cued by communications intelligence, the EO/IR sensor allowed the MARSS crew to track high-value individual targets on the move. Those individuals were then placed under surveillance using unmanned air vehicles (UAVs). Strikes could be called in and executed by fighters, strike fighters or even bomber aircraft.

Starting in 2006, MARSS went into combat with Task Force ODIN, an acronym for observe, detect, identify, and neutralise. The task force was dedicated to defeating IEDs, first in Iraq and then in Afghanistan.

In 2011, Afghanistan-based US Army SIGINT aircraft started to use a system called CAESAR, an acronym for communications attack, electronic surveillance, and reconnaissance. CAESAR could either monitor, jam or disrupt cell phones and radios, and incorporated electronic attack and electronic countermeasures capabilities.

MC-12 Liberty

The US Air Force was reluctant to improve its SIGINT force for the conflicts in Iraq and Afghanistan, even though the Department of Defense wanted more round-the-clock ISR coverage. The reluctance shown by senior US Air Force leaders escalated until it culminated with the sacking of the US Air Force Secretary Michael Wynne and its chief of staff, General Michael Moseley on June 5, 2008.

Their successors went ahead to introduce a new multi-spectral ISR aircraft with a good SIGINT capability. Orders were placed in July 2008, to commence procurement of what would become the MC-12W Liberty.

Experience of improvising and operating EC-47s in the Vietnam conflict had been largely forgotten by the US Air Force when the Department of Defense forced the service to procure the MC-12W. Getting the type into action quickly became the responsibility of the US Air Force's Big Safari programme office, one experienced in the modification and sustainment of special mission aircraft based at Wright-Patterson Air Force Base, Ohio.

Beechcraft King Air 350ERs were ordered and fitted with L3 Communications SIGINT and SATCOM systems, EO/IR sensors, and a laser illuminator and designator. A datalink was used to downlink sensor feeds directly to combat aircraft equipped with the Link-16 system or to troops using a laptop terminal hosting a remotely operated video enhanced receiver system dubbed ROVER.

Following a hasty training programme using scratch crews drawn from throughout the US Air Force, MC-12Ws first went into action over Iraq in June 2009 operated by the 362nd Expeditionary Reconnaissance Squadron based at Balad Air Base. MC-12 deliveries were supplemented by four civil-registered and contractor-operated Blue Devil twin-turboprop Beechcraft 90s in 2010.

Liberty in Combat

US Air Force MC-12Ws were operated by a two-person flight deck crew and an aft cabin mission crew.

On the flight deck, the mission commander and pilot would normally follow a pre-planned route, following country-wide operational priorities for ISR of which there was an insatiable demand to support ground operations.

Once the aircraft had spiralled up to its operational altitude (often over 18,000ft to reduce vulnerability to missile threats) and was trimmed out, the mission commander would often leave the flying to the pilot and manage the sensors using a screen, keyboard, and a mouse.

Racetrack patterns were flown on station to minimise the likelihood of sensors and antennas being blanked out by the wings during turns. During an aircraft-to-aircraft handover, the crew of the MC-12 aircraft arriving on station had to fly the pattern with the aircraft already there, because there was no way to transfer the monitoring already underway.

In a dynamic tactical situation, MC-12Ws could be re-tasked to work with other manned aircraft or

ABOVE • *RC-12P 92-13125 assigned to the Wiesbaden-based 1st Military Intelligence Battalion seen in July 2002. The RC-12P variant featured smaller and lighter wing tip pods.*
BOB ARCHER COLLECTION

UAVs, using the on-board laser target designator.

An MC-12 mission crew usually comprised a linguist responsible for intercepting and monitoring enemy voice transmissions, and a sensor operator.

Data could be transferred via datalink and SATCOM to a ground station, which had the capability to analyse and fuse information, and if required, to take over control of the aircraft's onboard sensors.

The hastily improvised MC-12W squadrons were able to successfully execute their missions, recording a 99.96% mission accomplishment rate in Afghanistan. This achievement can be attributed to the ability and professionalism of individual personnel, very few of whom had ISR experience, and training for ab initio personnel was limited. Short tours of duty meant that some 20% of personnel assigned to each deployed MC-12W squadron turned over every month. US Air Force personnel were supplemented by personnel from other services and civilian contractors.

Effects of its hasty development and deployment were also apparent during flight operations. It was only after an MC-12W, trying to climb over a storm cloud in Afghanistan, stalled and went into an unrecoverable spin, killing all

aboard, that it became apparent that neither the pilots nor indeed anyone in the US Air Force knew what the MC-12's stall speed was.

When fully loaded at altitude, the MC-12W had a more limited flight envelope than a King Air 350ER in standard configuration. For MC-12W pilots, the aircraft's handling was affected by the dorsal SATCOM radome and the ventral sensor pannier configuration.

Following the wind down of operational commitments in the US Central Command's area of responsibility after 2014, the US Air Force hustled the MC-12W out of service. Aircraft were transferred to other services, with just one squadron retained by Air Force Special Operations Command for ISR training and operational commitments held by US Southern Command.

RC-12 Guardrails

Often overlooked within its own service (the world's largest operator of helicopters), US Army ISR aircraft, in war and peace, have often been over-shadowed by larger four-engine US Air Force and US Navy SIGINT aircraft like the RC-135 Rivet Joint and EP-3E Aries II. But these aircraft have been involved everywhere American soldiers have

engaged in combat. They provided half of the in-country SIGINT capability in South Vietnam during the Vietnam war. More recently, US Army aircraft have been heavily committed to Afghanistan, Iraq, and Syria.

US Army SIGINT aircraft are intended to provide corps-level and other commanders with timely intelligence used to direct the fight and win the ground battle. During the advance on Baghdad in 2003, monitoring Iraqi tactical communications helped identify which roads were open or where ambushes were being prepared. In peacetime, US Army SIGINT aircraft help provide indications and warning (I&W) of potential threat activities.

The Guardrail system first entered US Army service in 1971. It linked three modified Beechcraft King Air Model 200s designated as RU-21s to an integrated signal processing facility at a decommissioned Nike surface-to-air missile (SAM) site at Grünstadt, West Germany. Up to 18 operators in 40ft trailers monitored what the aircraft were picking up in real time. Since then, successive versions of the RC-12 Guardrail operated along the border with the German Democratic Republic during the Cold War and parallel to the Korean demilitarised zone. In the 1990s, Guardrail aircraft were part of the NATO

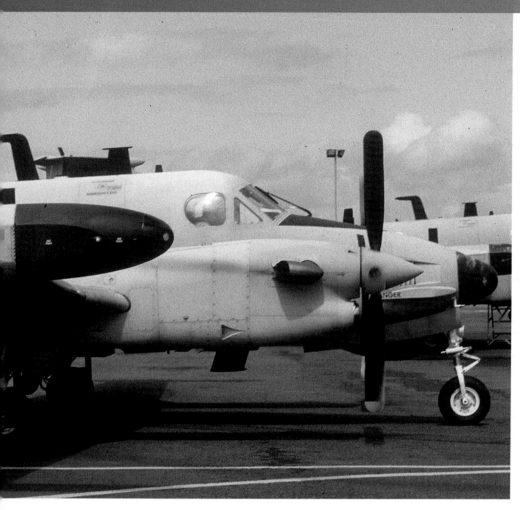

The first RC-12H (of 6) configured with the GRCS System 3 (Minus) and 15,000lb increased MTOW was delivered in 1988.

The first RC-12G (of 3) configured with the Crazy Horse system used to gather unique ELINT in Central America to counter insurgency and counter drug operations, and an a 15,000lb MTOW was delivered in 1985.

The first RC-12K (of 9) configured with the GRCS System 4, a large cargo door, more powerful PT6A-67 turboprops each rated at 1,100shp, oversized landing gear, and an increased 16,000lb MTOW was delivered in 1990.

The first RC-12N (of 15) configured with the GRCS System 1 was delivered in 1994.

The first RC-12P (of 9) configured with the GRCS System 2, a new different datalink, fibre optic cabling, smaller and lighter wing pods and an increased 16,500lb MTOW was delivered in 1999.

The first RC-12Q (of 3) was delivered in 1999. Dubbed the Direct Air Satellite Relay aircraft the variant was configured with a dorsal radome housing a satellite communications antenna to expand the aircraft's operational area outside satellite footprints compared to the RC-12P.

The first RC-12X (of 19) was delivered in 2011. The RC-12X is configured with an upgraded GRCS system that features SIGINT technology developed for the Block 30 RQ-4 Global Hawk, featuring expanded frequency ranges, a capability to locate signals in both stand-off and stand-in modes,

coalition of SIGINT aircraft conducting ISR missions over the former Yugoslavia.

A fleet of RC-12 aircraft replaced much older RU-21s, various models of which hosted the first generation of Guardrail systems.

The Improved Guardrail V (integrated on RC-12D aircraft) and the Guardrail Common Sensor (GRCS) systems are remotely controlled, airborne SIGINT collection and location systems.

The first RC-12D (of 13) configured with the ASD-9 Guardrail V remote-controlled communications intercept and direction-finding system was delivered in 1983.

and an adaptive beam-forming antenna array used to locate emitters in dense signal environments.

The RC-12X is the US Army's current integrated SIGINT platform that provides near real-time targeting information to tactical commanders and supports full-spectrum operations. The Guardrail system has been modernised since inception to maintain relevancy and to enable continued prosecution of emerging threats within changing battlespaces.

GRCS sensor capability produces COMINT and ELINT for battlefield mapping of common and modern signals of interest for detection, identification, and geolocation of known threats.

The standard concept of operations supports both single-ship, multi-ship and cooperative operations using tactical common data links (TCDL) and network-based infrastructure back through an operational ground station (OGS) and a Distributed Common Ground System-Army, located in the United States for correlation, exploitation, and dissemination.

RC-12X aircraft are former RC-12N and RC-12P models, upgraded by the Guardrail programme's prime contractor, Northrop Grumman. The upgrade included structural modifications, a digital cockpit, and integration of a Northrop Grumman sensor and communications suite, with datalinks and remote operating capability.

An RC-12X Guardrail aircraft is the air component of the GRCS system. The US Army has 14 RC-12X aircraft in operation, assigned to the two aerial exploitation units, the 3rd and 204th Military Intelligence Battalions. The 3rd MI BN(AE) is based at Camp Humphreys-

Desiderion Army Airfield, Pyongtaek, Republic of Korea, and the 204th MI BN(AE) at Fort Bliss-Biggs Army Airfield, El Paso, Texas.

Like their 1971 predecessors, multiple RC-12X aircraft normally operate together between 20,000 and 24,000ft to gather near-real time SIGINT and geolocation information. Data gathered is downlinked via a TCDL to a GRCS operational ground station.

In combat, the RC-12X can also conduct targeting, and is currently certified to undertake precision long-range fire support, netted into digital networks through the OGS and the US Army's variant of the distributed common ground system.

Current US Army ISR Fleet

The US Army operates dozens of turboprop-ISR aircraft, comprising RC-12X Guard Rails, MC-12S aircraft based on the Beechcraft King Air 350ER fitted with the Enhanced Medium Altitude Reconnaissance and Surveillance System (EMARSS) system (see below), and De Havilland Canada DHC-7-based EO-5s.

RC-12X Guardrail Common Sensor

The Guardrail Common Sensor (GRCS) is the heart of a special electronic mission aircraft with integrated COMINT and ELINT collection and reporting, enhanced signal classification and recognition, and precision emitter geolocation capabilities.

Guardrail was originally built as a Cold War system to provide indications and warnings against adversaries in both the European and Pacific Theatres of Operation.

The Guardrail system has been modernised since inception to maintain relevancy and to enable continued prosecution of emerging threats within the changing battlespace.

GRCS is hosted on a Beechcraft King Air B200 twin-engine turboprop aircraft, designated the RC-12X, and is the US Army's premiere airborne SIGINT-collection and precision targeting location system. The US Army currently operates a fleet of 14 RC-12X mission

BELOW • *An MC-12W assigned to the 137th Special Operations Wing, Oklahoma National Guard, taxies at San Angelo Regional Airport, Texas.* US AIR FORCE/ AIRMAN 1ST CLASS ZACHARY HEIMBUCH

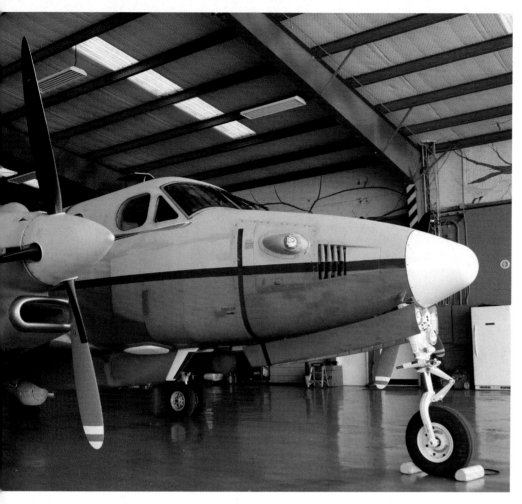

multi-ship and cooperative operations using tactical common data links and network-based infrastructure back to continental United States based garrisons where it is correlated, exploited, and disseminated to supported commands.

GRCS sensor capability produces high-accuracy communications intelligence (COMINT) and electronic intelligence (ELINT) for battlefield mapping of common and modern signals of interest for detection, identification, and geolocation of known threats. The system enables exploitation of common and modern signals through a large frequency band with precision accuracy.

Ground processing software and hardware are part of the US Army tactical SIGINT baseline which are interoperable with DCGS-A, OGS and CONUS garrison locations, a factor that reduces the deployed footprint at a forward location.

Planned improvements include technical refresh efforts for the ELINT and COMINT subsystems using software defined open architecture and cockpit avionics upgrades.

During FY2019, the US Army's Fixed Wing Project Office had completed an avionics upgrade to meet military and civilian requirements for communication, navigation, and surveillance to meet GATM requirements; enhanced the Mode-5 IFF capability; and integrated a moving map capability. During the following FY2020 and FY2021, the project office upgraded the UHF radios, and the GPS antennae to

aircraft, which are planned to remain in service until 2034 following a life extension in FY2018.

The Distributed Common Ground System–Army (DCGS-A) Operational Ground Station (OGS) processing, exploitation and dissemination capabilities allow for real-time signal

exploitation and reporting, to provide information dominance to commanders.

Data, payload tasking and mission operations support are provided by the 116th Military Intelligence Brigade at Fort Gordon, Georgia.

Guardrail's standard concept of operations supports both single-ship,

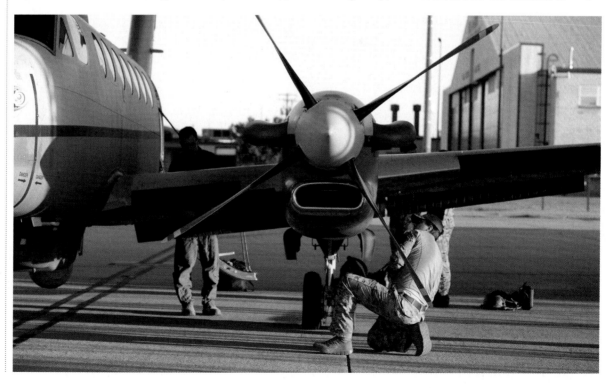

address Assured Positioning, Navigation and Timing (A-PNT) requirements.

The final RC-12X Guardrail missions were flown in the European Command area of responsibility on January 14, 2023. A contingent of RC-12X Guardrail aircraft were based at Šiauliai Air Base, Lithuania, and flew daily missions around the border of Belarus and the Russian enclave of Kaliningrad on the coast of the Baltic Sea. The Guardrail aircraft were operated by the 204th Military Intelligence Battalion based at Biggs Army Airfield in El Paso, Texas. The Šiauliai-based detachment operated between December 2019 and January 2023.

The RC-12X fleet comprises five trainer aircraft used by the 305th Military Intelligence Battalion based at Fort Huachuca, Arizona and 14 operational aircraft. The trainers are not equipped with a full suite of sensors.

MC-12S EMARSS

The MC-12S EMARSS provides a persistent airborne intelligence, surveillance, and reconnaissance capability to detect, locate, classify, identify, and track surface targets with a high degree of timeliness and accuracy during day, night, and nearly all-weather conditions. It is designed to enhance the effectiveness of a Brigade Combat Team by defining and assessing the communications environment and providing surveillance, targeting support, and threat warning.

The system has a tailored set of Distributed Common Ground System – Army (DCGS-A) enabled software ISR functionalities to process, exploit, and rapidly disseminate the intelligence derived from the sensor capabilities.

Selected EMARSS intelligence data is immediately processed on the aircraft and forwarded to a DCGS-A for further processing, analysis, and reporting.

EMARSS complies with Department of Defense (DoD) Information Technology Standards Registry and Defense Information Systems Network. This architecture enables interoperability with any multiservice or joint system that complies with DoD standard formats for data transfer and dissemination.

EMARSS enables the Aerial Exploitation Battalions within the US Army's Intelligence and Security Command to provide command and control, mission planning, sustainment support, and deployment packages to facilitate worldwide missions in accordance with standard Joint and US Army tasking processes.

The EMARSS is configured to four standards each with specific capability.

- EMARSS-G gathers geospatial intelligence with wide area aerial surveillance, light detection and ranging, and high-definition full motion video (HD FMV) capabilities.
- EMARSS-M gathers multi-intelligence with signals intelligence and HD FMV capabilities.

LEFT • *An MC-12W assigned to the 137th Special Operations Wing, Oklahoma National Guard, taxies across the flightline at Will Rogers Air National Guard Base, Oklahoma City.* US AIR NATIONAL GUARD/TSGT BRIGETTE WALTERMIRE

• EMARSS-V has a vehicle and dismount exploitation radar (VADER) with vehicle and dismount moving target indication, signals intelligence, and HD FMV capabilities.
• EMARSS-S gathers signals intelligence with broad spectrum signals intelligence and HD FMV capabilities.

The Army Acquisition Objective for EMARSS is 36 systems, with an Army Procurement Objective of 24, to include the following variants: eight EMARSS-G; four EMARSS-V; eight EMARSS-M; and four EMARSS-S. Congress also approved funding for up to two additional EMARSS-E aircraft.

The budget supports the conversion of Special Electronic Mission Aircraft and Liberty Project aircraft into Enhanced Medium Altitude Reconnaissance and Surveillance Systems. The budget provides for the procurement of replacement and spare engines, procurement and associated testing of civil and military aircraft equipment,

and the integration of an ISR mission equipment package.

During FY2019, the US Army's Fixed Wing Project Office had completed integration and initial fielding of the redesigned operator workstation computer and completed integration, testing, and first article installation of the Airborne Wide Area Persistent Surveillance System (AWAPSS) Obsolescence Improvement Program and associated common rack. This was followed in FY2021 and FY2022 by addressing SIGINT sensor obsolescence for the EMARSS-M.

The project office is continuing with its effort to implement a high priority capability called the Assured Positioning, Navigation and Timing, aircraft survivability equipment and performance upgrades, conduct SIGINT sensor, software, and architecture upgrades for EMARSS-S, and develop synthetic aperture radar/moving target indicator upgrade to address obsolescence in the VADER system.

MC-12S EMARSS-V

On June 30, 2020, the US Army took delivery of the first upgraded EMARSS–Vehicle and Dismount Exploitation Radar (EMARRS-V) prototype at the Sierra Nevada Corporation Hagerstown, Maryland facility.

The US Army Contracting Command – Redstone, on behalf of the Fixed Wing Project Office, awarded a contract to Sierra Nevada Corporation for the modification of one EMARSS-V aircraft as a prototype in September 2019. During the $5m, seven-month undertaking, systems were integrated to enhance performance, increase safety, and improve the aircraft's ability to operate in a near-peer environment.

Colonel James DeBoer, fixed wing project manager said: "The modified EMARSS-V aircraft has more powerful engines which allow for better performance at higher elevations and hotter temperatures during take-off. It can operate out of a wider range of airfields because it uses less runway for take-off. A larger fuel capacity

allows this aircraft to stay airborne longer for its ISR missions. With these improvements, the EMARSS-V prototype will allow US Army aviation to more effectively support Joint All-Domain Operations/Multi-Domain Operations."

The EMARSS-V aircraft received a modernisation upgrade and completed its final flight testing on May 27, 2020. The modernisation upgrade provided the aircraft with an Anti-Jam/Selective Availability Anti-Spoofing Module Global Positioning System, Automatic Dependent Surveillance-Broadcast functionality with encrypted APX-119 Mode 5 Level 2 transponder, improved situational awareness with the existing Blue Force Tracker-2, incorporation of the Avalex ACM9454 cockpit management unit, and the installation of the mission enhancement kit that will result in increased safety, greater mission capability, increased mission performance and fewer basing limitations.

The installed mission enhancement kit (MEK) comprises higher performance PT6A-67A engines, lightweight composite propellers, a lightweight lithium-ion battery, and an anti-lock braking system. The MEK reduces aircraft weight while increasing take-off performance in high/hot environments. In addition, the anti-lock braking system reduces take-off field length which increases the number of suitable airfields where this modernised EMARSS-V can operate. Operational data from the EMARSS fleet indicates that an aircraft's endurance is reduced by approximately two hours when using current engines in high/hot conditions. The increased

capability provided by the MEK allows unit commanders to increase fuel capacity which in turn increases the aircraft's overall endurance during critical intelligence, surveillance, and reconnaissance operations.

The EMARSS-V prototype was inducted at Fort Hood, Texas with the 15th Military Intelligence Battalion in July and then ferried to the L3 Harris facility in Greenville, Texas for scheduled maintenance. The aircraft flew to the Command, Control, Computers, Communications, Cyber, Intelligence, Surveillance and Reconnaissance Flight Activity facility at Lakehurst, New Jersey to undergo calibration and testing of the SIGINT system. On completion of testing, the aircraft returned to the 15th Military Intelligence Battalion for operational tasking.

Two EMARSS-Electronic Intelligence (EMARSS-E) prototype aircraft are under development, and these will have the capability of intercepting, direction finding, and geolocation of emitters, and support of All-domain Overhead Cooperative Operations.

EO-5C ARL

A small fleet of highly-modified De Havilland Canada DHC-7 aircraft, designated EO-5Cs are configured with the multi-sensor, day and night, all-weather Aerial Intelligence, Surveillance, Reconnaissance system, awkwardly named Airborne Reconnaissance Low-Multifunction or ARL-M.

An ARL aircraft provides tactical commanders with day and night, all-weather, real-time airborne COMINT/IMINT collection, and a designated area surveillance system. The reconfigurable

payload provides flexibility to the commander. ARL provides real-time down-link of actionable intelligence to Brigade Combat Teams and higher echelons across the full range of military operations.

Equipment installed on ARL aircraft comprises: Dual EO/IR day/night high-definition full motion video sensors with laser range finding and target

ABOVE • The modifications made to a baseline King Air 350 to configure the aircraft to MC-12S EMARSS standard can be seen in this photo. SIERRA NEVADA CORPORATION

designation capability; tactical signals and communication intelligence/direction finding subsystems with theatre net-centric geolocation; synthetic aperture radar and ground/dismount-moving target indicator radar; hyperspectral imagery/long-range radar and short-range radar; and DCGS-A enabled workstations.

Next Steps

Rather than fund the GRCS, the US Army awarded a contract to MAG Aerospace and L3Harris to deliver two Bombardier Global 6500 aircraft, modified for the Army Theatre Level, High-Altitude Expeditionary Next Airborne programmes known as ATHENA-R (radar) and ATHENA-S (SIGINT).

The ARTEMIS-R aircraft will be equipped with a synthetic aperture radar with ground moving target tracking capability, and the ARTEMIS-S aircraft will be fitted with a signals detection system.

Under the Airborne Reconnaissance Targeting Exploitation Mission Intelligence System (ARTEMIS) programme launched in 2019, prime contractor Leidos has developed a sensor suite featuring its High-Accuracy Detection and Exploitation System (HADES). This is an airborne component

of the Multi-Domain Sensing System (MDSS), intended to enable multi-domain operations, with COMINT, ELINT and geolocations capabilities.

Currently the programme uses two contractor owned/contractor operated Bombardier CL-600 Challenger 650 business jets to demonstrate operational utility while minimising the US Army's up-front investment.

In July 2020, the Challenger 650 flew to Kadena Air Base, Okinawa to fly missions. In August, ARTEMIS was revealed to the public and in September one of the Challengers deployed to Georgia to participate, with other US forces, in Exercise Noble Partner. In November 2021, an ARTEMIS-configured aircraft participating in experiments under Project Convergence at the Yuma Proving Grounds in Arizona was re-tasked to deploy to Europe to join the NATO operation to monitor Russian military forces amassing near the Ukraine border.

Applicable Lessons?

In the future, it is likely that sensors will be improvised to counter the challenges presented by emerging threats rather than using fleets of ever more advanced ISR aircraft. Sensors are being

developed as modular systems, often pod mounted, with software designed to enable a plug and play capability, in theory removing lengthy and expensive development cycles.

Although pod-mounted systems have given tactical aircraft a SIGINT collection capability since their introduction in the 1960s, today the miniaturisation of SIGINT systems dictates what changes can and will be made in the future. Miniaturisation means that UAVs can be used for such missions, while the use of smaller, specialised manned aircraft including the EMARSS and Shadow R2 will provide operational flexibility.

Allied and coalition air arms have discovered that twin-engine turboprop and business jet airframes fitted with integrated sensor suites and datalinks give them many of the capabilities provided by larger and more expensive systems such as Rivet Joint for a fraction of their procurement and operating costs.

The time to invest in such platforms is before any conflict forces urgent improvisations. Comparing the rise and fall of the EC-47 and MC-12W in US Air Force service, with the steady tailored refinement of US Army twin-engine SIGINT aircraft supports that assertion.

BELOW • *An MC-12S EMARSS.* SIERRA NEVADA CORPORATION

SUBSCRIBE

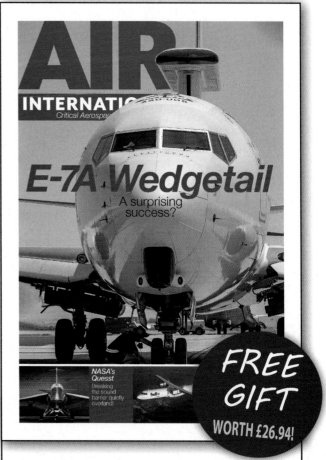
ORDER DIRECT FROM OUR SHOP...
shop.keypublish

OR CALL +44 (0)1780 480404

(Lines open 9.00-5.30, Monday-Friday GMT)

KEY
Publishin

827/23

TODAY

BACK ON TOUR HMS QUEEN ELIZABETH

AIRFORCES MONTHLY

OFFICIALLY THE WORLD'S NUMBER ONE AUTHORITY ON MILITARY AVIATION

Exclusive!

RAF Fighter Force

The busiest in Europe?

Guns for Hire
Mercenary aviators in west Africa

From pirates to Putin
On patrol with German naval aviation

Pakistan's retired recce Mirages

Spang's Wild Weasels
F-16s bite into Cobra Warrior

Russia's dismal Frogfoots
No way back for the underperforming Su-25

FREE GIFT WORTH £17.98!

TEHRAN NEXT? IRAN'S AIR DEFENSES

COMBAT AIRCRAFT JOURNAL

AMERICA'S BEST SELLING MILITARY AVIATION MAGAZINE

VENGEANCE

ISRAEL LOOKING TO CRUSH HAMAS BUT AT WHAT COST?

KEEPING IRAN AND HEZBOLLAH IN CHECK
US aircraft carriers' *Ford* and *Eisenhower* sent to eastern Med

FREE GIFT WORTH £17.99!

Airforces Monthly is devoted entirely to modern military aircraft and their air arms.

shop.keypublishing.com/afmsubs

Combat Aircraft Journal is renowned for being America's best-selling military aviation magazine.

shop.keypublishing.com/casubs

ing.com

ARIES II

Mark Ayton reviews the US Navy's EP-3E Aries fleet of multi-intelligence reconnaissance aircraft.

An EP-3E is an extensively modified P-3 Orion fitted with the Airborne Reconnaissance Integrated Electronic System dubbed ARIES. Originally introduced to fleet service in 1971 and configured for signals intelligence (SIGINT), today the EP-3E is classed as a multi-intelligence reconnaissance aircraft with a much-improved SIGINT and full motion video capability. According to Naval Air Systems Command, the EP-3E is equipped with sensitive receivers and high-gain dish antennas used for the exploitation of a wide range of electronic emissions

from deep within targeted territory while operating in international airspace. The crew fuses the collected intelligence along with off-board data and disseminates the collaborated information for direct threat warning, indications and warnings, information dominance, battle space situational awareness, suppression of enemy air defences, destruction of enemy air-defence, anti-air warfare and anti-submarine warfare applications. Additionally, an EP-3E's crew gathers technical information and intelligence about weapon systems in use by potential adversary nations.

The first ten EP-3Es were modified P-3A-model Orion maritime patrol aircraft configured to ARIES I standard. These were replaced by 12 former P-3Cs modified to the new generation ARIES II standard. Lockheed undertook modification of the first five aircraft between 1986 and 1991 at its Greenville, South Carolina facility, when the programme was transferred to the Naval Air Depots at Alameda, California and Jacksonville, Florida. EP-3E ARIES II BuNo 156507 made the type's first flight from Greenville on April 11, 1990. The last ARIES II aircraft entered fleet service in 1997.

Q-birds

The current and probably last home station for the US Navy EP-3E Aries II is Naval Air Station Whidbey Island, Washington.

Whidbey-based Fleet Air Reconnaissance Squadron One (VQ-1) 'World Watchers' is the last remnant of a community that has collected SIGINT and provided early warning since the 1950s. VQ-1, having grown from the absorption of VQ-2, operates ten EP-3E ARIES II aircraft, with large crews comprising evaluators, intercept operators and linguists who deploy worldwide, often in response to tasking from national command authorities. Colloquially, EP-3E ARIES II aircraft are referred to as Q-birds, a term derived from the VQ squadron designation.

During the early 1990s, the Conversion-in-Lieu-of-Procurement programme converted 12 P-3Cs to EP-3E ARIES II configuration, using in part mission systems transferred from two EP-3B and the ten original EP-3E ARIES I aircraft.

An EP-3E is manned by a crew of up to 24 comprising three pilots,

BELOW • *A rare night-time shot of two EP-3E ARIES II aircraft on the flight line at Naval Air Station Whidbey Island, Washington, the home station of VQ-1.*
MATTHEW CLEMENTS

LEFT • *EP-3E ARIES II BuNo 156511 taxiing out to the runway at Naval Support Authority Souda Bay, Crete in August 2017 showing all four radomes atop and the fuselage underside.* MATTHEW CLEMENTS

one electronic warfare aircraft navigator (EWAN), one flight engineer, an electronic warfare aircraft commander (EWAC), a senior electronic warfare tactical evaluator (SEVAL), a mission commander and two electronic warfare operators.

The EWAC datalinks intelligence information directly to all commanders. The EWAN maintains the aircraft's position and navigation throughout the mission. The SEVAL manages mission planning, collection, and reporting requirements, determines the tactical scenario based on SIGINT available and compiles operational intelligence reports for use by all commanders.

BELOW • *Three VQ-1 EP-3E ARIES II aircraft share a flight line at Naval Air Station Whidbey Island with a grey P-3C Orion. The proximity to camera of aircraft 325 shows some of the aircraft's antennas and radomes.* MATTHEW CLEMENTS

ARIES Upgrades

The EP-3E has gone through several upgrades to increase its capabilities. In 2003, Naval Air Systems Command's Maritime Patrol and Reconnaissance Aircraft (MPRA) program office PMA-290, began the JCC upgrade to incrementally improve the EP-3E's SIGINT sensor system capabilities. JCC refers to the awkwardly named Joint airborne SIGINT architecture modernization Common Configuration.

Commenting, a PMA-290 official said: "JCC upgrades provided the navy with an automated electronic surveillance measures capability, connectivity to the classified airborne ForceNET network, precision direction finding, low-band multiplatform geo-location communications collection, recording and information operations capabilities."

The JCC upgrade package was first installed on the final five P-3C aircraft modified to EP-3E configuration, followed by each of the other seven in fleet service as they went through depot maintenance or special structural inspections. The first EP-3E configured with the JCC entered fleet service in 2005.

Both the JCC and another modification known as Task Force Intelligence, Surveillance and Reconnaissance (TF-ISR) included hardware and software upgrades that aligned the EP-3E with the

navy's cryptologic architecture. These mods bridged the gap between its present capabilities and future manned/ unmanned reconnaissance aircraft, and integrated Link-16 mission management capabilities.

Another modification, known as the Sensor System Improvement Program (SSIP) upgraded the type's communication suite, and enhanced signals intelligence collection and data-automation capabilities.

According to Naval Air Systems Command, the SSIP passed an operational assessment by the commander, Operational Test and Evaluation Force in September 2004

and found SSIP to be operationally effective and suitable, a significant improvement in capability over previous versions, and was recommended for fleet introduction.

Developmental testing of SSIP occurred in FY2003 split between the software integration lab at the Raytheon Technical Services Company facility in Indianapolis, Indiana and by NAVAIR at Naval Air Station Patuxent River, Maryland.

In 2007, PMA-290 implemented upgrades of the EP-3E's electro-optical/ infrared (EO/IR) and ForceNET systems to meet emerging TF-ISR requirements. This effort included installation of a

turret under the forward fuselage, improved international maritime satellite connectivity, additional special signals boxes and line-of-sight wide-band data links for full-motion video.

During 2010, L-3 Communications delivered a prototype EP-3E configured with its Spiral 3 modification for operational testing. L-3's Spiral 3 fit comprised an upgraded ISR mission avionics suite featuring a new communications intelligence (COMINT) equipment, new sensors, and improved network capabilities.

Used on a mission, the modifications improved onboard data analysis and enabled real-time tactical intelligence

ABOVE • *October 2008: VQ-1 EP-3E ARIES II BuNo 157325 at RAF Mildenhall, England in an earlier configuration, fitted with many more antennas under the outboard wings and the under fuselage, to aircraft 529 from October 2016.* LINDSAY PEACOCK

dissemination. Spiral 3 was under its operational test during 2011 leading to a full-rate production decision under which L-3 manufactured and installed the suite on three EP-3E aircraft.

Because of obsolescence, PMA-290 also began to upgrade the EP-3E's electronic surveillance measures in 2016.

To comply with Federal Aviation Administration airspace regulations, the EP-3E fleet was modified under the Communications, Navigation and Surveillance/Air Traffic Management programme. EP-3Es have been updated with a new communications suite, the protected instrument landing system, identification friend-or-foe Mode S, traffic collision avoidance system, and the required navigation performance enhancements including GPS and ADS-B capability.

The US Navy is keeping the EP-3E modernised until the end of its service life by replacing capabilities resident in the aircraft, which is no small chore. Eventually the navy will transition many of the EP-3E's capabilities to the MQ-4C Triton unmanned aerial system.

Still Going Strong

In 2023, the ruggedness of the EP-3E is evident by its ongoing operation with the US Navy conducting a type of mission that the P-3 was not originally designed to conduct, but that it has nevertheless done very effectively. For 20 years, navy EP-3s were heavily tasked with Cold War operations, every conflict since, and a lot of clandestine work that remains classified. Lockheed EP-3s replaced Lockheed EC-121Ms.

The first two EP-3B aircraft entered service with VQ-1 in 1969. The first EP-3E ARIES I aircraft was assigned to the fleet in 1991. The type served until it was replaced with ARIES II standard aircraft between 1991 and 1997. Even though the same airframes remain in navy service today, their mission systems have changed considerably. Not least because Chinese specialists were able to analyse the systems on board aircraft BuNo 156511 following the most famous EP-3E mission ever.

On April 1, 2001, aircraft BuNo 156511 survived a mid-air collision with a People's Liberation Army Naval Air Force J-8 fighter and diverted to Lingshui Air Base on Hainan Island. The aircraft was very badly damaged and eventually dismantled by a Lockheed Martin recovery team and airlifted back to the United States where it was re-built.

Operators from all the US armed services who operate the EP-3E as mission crew liked the ARIES system because it fully-integrates data from across the RF spectrum, provides real-time battlespace situational awareness, and records signals for post-mission technical analysis.

Fleet commanders appreciate having an EP-3E airborne because of the flexibility held by the crew that enables them to easily switch reconnaissance tasking when new and tactically significant information is prosecuted. Intelligence that commanders need to know about. Furthermore, an EP-3E's architecture can be reconfigured by the squadron at its home station or forward operating base. A beneficial attribute for dealing with a real-world scenario, and one that has paid off many times.

RIGHT • *Aviation Technicians prepare an EP-3E ARIES II for routine maintenance procedures at Naval Support Activity Souda Bay, Crete during a detachment to the US 6th Fleet area of operations.* US NAVY/HEATHER JUDKINS

Unmanned Maritime Surveillance

Mark Ayton spoke with the MQ-4C Triton programme representatives based at Naval Air Stations Patuxent River, Maryland and Jacksonville, Florida to learn about this fascinating unmanned aerial system.

In September 2023, Unmanned Patrol Squadron 19 (VUP-19) deployed MQ-4C Triton unmanned aerial vehicles to Andersen Air Force Base, Guam for the type's second deployment to the Pacific theatre for initial operations testing. The squadron previously deployed to Andersen and operated in the US 7th Fleet area of responsibility between January 2020 and October 2022.

Throughout the first deployment, VUP-19 operated two aircraft in the baseline configuration known as Integrated Functional Capability 3 (IFC 3) and commenced the development of tactics, techniques, and procedures for MQ-4C operations during ISR tasking issued by Commander, Task Force 72, the lead for patrol, reconnaissance, and surveillance forces in the 7th Fleet.

Aircrew and maintainers assigned to VUP-19 were deployed to Guam, with squadron leadership and mission operators remaining at Naval Air Station Jacksonville, Florida.

Andersen Air Force Base was VUP-19's primary deployed operating base with expeditionary deployments made

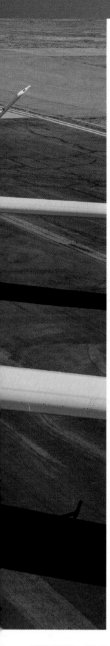

to two bases in Japan: Misawa Air Base and Marine Corps Air Station Iwakuni. The deployments to Japan were staged to refine the concept of operations for expeditionary basing, exercising the US Navy's requirement to operate from multiple sites within the 7th Fleet area of operations.

VUP-19 is operating and maintaining multiple MQ-4C air vehicles from Andersen as part of its initial operational capability (IOC) [designed to deliver signals intelligence (SIGINT) capability], to provide around-the-clock maritime intelligence, surveillance, reconnaissance and targeting (MISR-T) operations in the Indo-Pacific region. The MQ-4C air vehicles involved in the deployment are configured to the upgraded IFC4 standard featuring an enhanced multi-mission sensor capability, part of the US Navy's Maritime Intelligence, Surveillance, Reconnaissance and Targeting (MISR&T) transition plan.

According to Commander, Naval Air Forces: "These enhancements [IFC 4] increase Triton's ability to provide a persistent MISR-T capability alongside the P-8A Poseidon as a key component of the US Navy's Maritime Patrol and Reconnaissance Force family of systems (FoS)."

The first MQ-4C Triton unmanned aerial vehicle arrived at VUP-19's home station, Naval Air Station Mayport,

Florida, on December 16, 2021. It was one of two Triton aircraft that had operated from Naval Air Facility Misawa, after completion of the type's first rotational deployment to Japan on October 12, 2021, and Andersen.

At the time, VUP-19 operated and maintained two MQ-4C aircraft as part of an early operational capability (EOC) to refine the concept of operations, including expeditionary basing, and complement manned systems [primarily the P-8A Poseidon] to better locate, identify, and track contacts of interest in the maritime domain.

Patuxent River's Integrated Test Team

Located in a purpose-built facility on board Naval Air Station Patuxent River, the Triton Integrated Test Team (ITT) is equipped with three air vehicles, a hangar wide enough to house all three aircraft wingtip to wingtip (an MQ-4C has a 130ft 10in wingspan) and each type of control station required for its ongoing flight test programme including those to be used at forward operating sites.

It's worth noting that the Triton ITT comprises personnel from both the developmental and operational test authorities based at Patuxent River: Air Test and Evaluation Squadron 20 (VX-20) and Air Test and Evaluation Squadron1 (VX-1) 'Pioneers', respectively.

There are many aspects to the MQ-4C Triton and its missions. Some are fascinating. Based on the Northrop Grumman RQ-4 Global Hawk, the MQ-4C looks very similar, but looks can deceive. Under the skin, the MQ-4C has strengthened wing structures and an anti-ice and de-icing system, and a suite of systems all of which make the US Navy variant different from its US Air Force brethren.

Operational Assessment

Throughout the second half of 2015 the Triton ITT and PMA-262 were busy with the integration effort of software load IFC 2.2, the configuration required for the Triton system's first operational assessment (OA). This event was designed to provide the ITT and PMA-262 with information to help guide the focus of continued testing leading up to the operational evaluation period. Conducted between November 2015 and January 2016, the OA involved six flights, the longest of which was over 12-hours in duration, and about 60 hours of flight time testing Triton's envelope performance and its sensor suite comprising:

• A ZPY-3 multi-function active sensor active electronically steered array (MFAS AESA) maritime surveillance radar designed to detect, identify, and track surface targets and produce high-resolution imagery.

ABOVE AND RIGHT • MQ-4C Triton aircraft, BuNo 168457 and 168458, at Northrop Grumman's test facility in Palmdale, California. US NAVY/ NORTHROP GRUMMAN/ CHAD SLATTERY

ABOVE • *MQ-4C Triton BuNo 168457 during an early test flight from Palmdale California. This image clearly shows the configuration of the aft fuselage, engine, and vertical stabilisers.*
US NAVY/NORTHROP GRUMMAN/CHAD SLATTERY

• A DAS-3 MTS-B electro-optical/ infrared sensor to capture full motion video and still imagery of surface targets (the air vehicle's camera).
• A ZLQ-1 electronic support measures system which detects, identifies, and geo-locates radar threat signals.
• An automatic identification system (AIS) receiver which permits the detection, identification, geolocation, and tracking of cooperative maritime vessels equipped with AIS transponders.

Operationally representative in its construct, the OA also enabled the Triton ITT to test the on-board line-of-sight and beyond line-of-sight datalink and transfer systems, which provide air vehicle command and control

and transmit sensor data from the air vehicle to the mission control stations for dissemination to fleet tactical operation centres and intelligence exploitation sites.

Over the course of the six flights, crews were able to get Triton on station effectively and provide real-time updates to the navy end user. Crews found ways to improve functionality for fleet operators using procedural changes and identifying tweaks to the software to build a better user interface. One example was the reduction in the number of command pushes required for a certain function.

During the six flights, flight test crews looked at the stability of the sensors; the functional capability of the camera system; the full suite of communication

systems (radio, line-of-sight, and satellite); and checked sensors, communications and interoperability with a simulated surface combatant using the Surface Aviation Integration Laboratory (SAIL) at Patuxent River. The SAIL was also used to simulate different types of US Navy aircraft – the P-8A Poseidon was one example - to simulate interoperability with Triton in the mission sets conducted during the six flights.

Test crews evaluated their ability to detect a certain size of vessel using the DAS-3 camera; to detect and identify the type of ship from range using the ZPY-3 radar; determined the range at which they could detect a small fishing boat or a patrol craft versus the range at which they could detect and develop

RIGHT • *At the final approach fix, the air vehicle's system switches to glide scope mode, and lines the aircraft up on the centre of the runway.*
US NAVY/NORTHROP GRUMMAN/CHAD SLATTERY

the position, course, and speed of a larger merchant combatant ship.

A noteworthy aspect of the Triton system is its objective capability to fly missions up to 24 hours in duration at altitudes above 52,000ft to enable its mission systems to monitor two million square miles of ocean and coastal areas at a time.

The 2016 OA demonstrated an initial assessment of the ability to get an MQ-4C Triton on station effectively and provide real-time updates to the navy end user via the on-board line-of-sight and beyond-line-of-sight datalink and transfer systems.

Post-OA, the ITT conducted an initial assessment to allow PMA-262 and Northrop Grumman to improve the system's functionality, and numerous upgrades have been made to the system including building a better user interface with improvements to the displays.

In June 2016, the ITT team undertook the first missions to expand Triton's heavy weight envelope to a full fuel payload; a critical requirement if the MQ-4C is to attain a 24-hour flight duration. On the first mission a Triton, in heavy weight configuration, completed all test objectives while operating in a 20,000ft altitude band followed by a second flight operating in a 30,000ft altitude band. Since then, the ITT and PMA-262 has successfully

attained mission durations longer than 24 hours at altitudes above 52,000ft in heavy weight configuration.

Ground test activity started with IFC 3.1 in January 2017. This software load included improvements to functionality of the ZPY-3 radar (temperature management), DAS-3 MTS-B sensor (control), ZLQ-1 electronic support measures system (interface), AIS and basic communications relay. The improvements allowed the MQ-4C to achieve EOC and deliver a huge swath of sea surface coverage to operational commanders.

Operating Triton

The US Navy's Triton concept of operations (CONOPS) is to have an air vehicle operating thousands of miles away from the control station, two of which are planned at two locations: Naval Air Station Jacksonville, Florida and Naval Air Station Whidbey Island, Washington.

At Patuxent River, things differ to the fleet's CONOPS simply because the control stations are co-located with the aircraft, which means the air vehicle operator (AVO) can operate as the local crew with the aircraft (UA) or as the remote crew. In fleet service there will be two disparate crews: one on detachment with the UA and a mission control station at the forward operating base (FOB) and one back at the main operating base (MOB).

Like any other aircraft, a Triton mission starts with mission planning and preparation work between the crew, which comprises an AVO who is also the UAC (unmanned aircraft commander), a tactical coordinator (TACCO) and two mission payload operators (MPOs). The AVO has responsibility for the safe flight of the aircraft and its positioning for the tactical employment of the sensors; the TACCO is responsible for coordinating the tactical picture; and the MPOs

operate the sensors from their control stations. All members of the crew have pre-flight duties.

Before the aircraft is spotted (the colloquial term for parking the aircraft on a specific spot on the flight line) the crew commence mission briefings covering the safety, specific items, tasks, and goals of the day as well as the particulars needed for the pre-flight.

Teams then start their respective duties whether at the aircraft or at their control station. At Patuxent River, the UAC goes to the aircraft to conduct a walk around for pre-flight. That's unique, because in the fleet the aircraft is at the FOB. The difference between ops at Patuxent River and the fleet's CONOPS is the UAC will be at the MOB and will have to delegate the walk around to the local AVO, someone who is qualified to do that at the FOB. At Patuxent River, the UAC is with the aircraft.

ABOVE • *The first MQ-4C Triton made the type's inaugural cross-country ferry flight from Palmdale, California to Naval Air Station Patuxent River, Maryland overnight on September 17-18, 2014.* NAVAL AIR SYSTEMS COMMAND/ERIK HILDEBRANDT

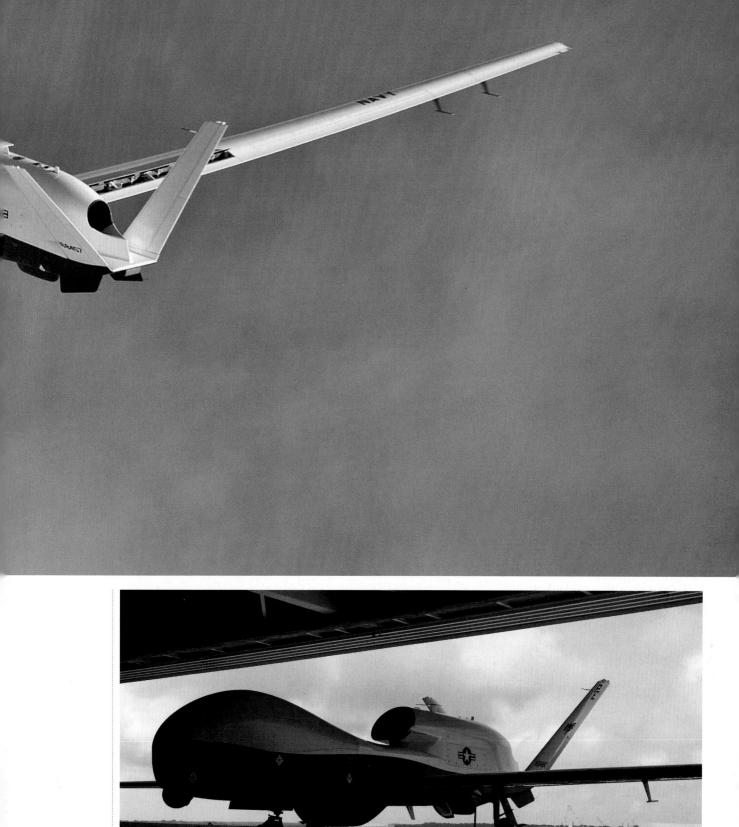

RIGHT • *MQ-4C Triton BuNo 168460/PE in the hangar at Andersen Air Force Base after arriving for the EOC deployment. The aircraft has the tail markings of Unmanned Patrol Squadron 19 (VUP-19).* US AIR FORCE/SENIOR AIRMAN RYAN BROOKS

Once the UAC has completed the walk around, the aircraft is handed over to the test controller, the person who ensures everything is buttoned up and secured on the aircraft. The UAC then goes to maintenance control to sign what's called the A sheet - the flight release - and takes responsibility for the aircraft as released by the maintenance department.

As mentioned earlier, the Triton system differs to a conventional aircraft in several ways, not least its mission duration. Flying for over 24 hours requires the crew to swap for each of the mission's multiple phases to ensure safe operation throughout. In fact, the navy has had to adjust its operating procedures to allow for a change of the aircraft's commander in flight. The original or previous UAC, the original signatory for the aircraft, ensures the next UAC signs a new A sheet to take responsibility for the aircraft during his or her phase of the mission. This handover process continues until the aircraft lands. In fleet ops the handover process is not so straightforward because the UAC is at the MOB and the aircraft is at the FOB. Devising a procedure for such a handover is a detail the Triton fleet

integration team continues to refine during the ongoing detached ops from Andersen Air Force Base.

Mission Control Stations

Two mission control stations (MCS) are used for all flight operations: a FOB MCS and a MOB MCS. The intent for the AVO at the FOB, who is within line-of-sight of the aircraft, is to control the aircraft on the ground, perform the take-off and the initial climb-out. He or she will then hand control of the aircraft over to the MOB. All control stations can control the aircraft and maintain command and control of the aircraft simultaneously. The intent of the CONOPS is for the FOB AVO to release command and control once it's under the control of the MOB whose crews fly the mission. Upon return to base, the aircraft is handed back to the FOB AVO for the final decent, landing and ground taxi input.

Autonomous Taxi

The AVO controls the air vehicle using a keyboard, a mouse, and a mission plan. The latter is developed and built from the start spot to the shutdown spot, the so-called spot-to-spot. Commands

BELOW • *MQ-4C Triton BuNo 168460/PE taxies at Andersen Air Force Base.* US AIR FORCE/SENIOR AIRMAN MICHAEL MURPHY

BELOW • US AIR FORCE/
SENIOR AIRMAN
MICHAEL MURPHY

given to the aircraft by the AVO are straightforward: taxi execute, stop execute, and take-off execute. Once taxi execute is given the aircraft taxies to the runway autonomously in accordance with the mission plan's route.

If the AVO commands the aircraft to taxi it will taxi. If the air vehicle loses control from the control station it will automatically stop, and the AVO can stop the taxi at any time. When the air vehicle takes the runway, it will not take-off unless it's given

a direct command from one of the two control stations. Automatic logic is built into the air vehicle's control system and has most significance in the event of an aborted take-off. A manual abort command is also available to the AVO faced with such an incident.

Working with the air vehicle crew during taxi and take-off is a second crew driving a ground chase vehicle. The crew in the vehicle watch for obstructions, and other aircraft or airfield traffic in the way. They are in constant radio contact with the control stations. When the aircraft takes the

runway, the car also takes the runway. When the aircraft releases the brakes, the driver accelerates as best they can to keep up with the aircraft, almost like a formation take-off. When the aircraft lifts off, the car exits the runway. The aircraft lifts off at just over 100kts depending on its weight and can abort at take-off speeds between 90 and 100kts.

For landing, the car crew is given a warning. The driver sets up at the end of the runway holding short. As soon as the aircraft passes the car, the driver follows the aircraft in almost a formation landing. The car crew run take-off

Control When Airborne

Once airborne, the aircraft follows its mission plan route. Local air traffic control (ATC) has details of the route because it can be close to, or different to the local departure and arrival patterns. What's more interesting about ATC coordination is manual flying which requires extra coordination because there is no one on board the aircraft to look out for other traffic. The air vehicle crew works with ATC just like any other aircraft and remain in communication with the controller to ensure the aircraft remains in a safe position, especially in the event of any kind of malfunction.

The mission plan and its route are created for autonomous control; the aircraft autonomously follows the route and executes all instructions within the plan.

However, the crew can manually control the aircraft at any time using different commands. Examples include limiting the altitude while the air vehicle continues to follow the mission plan

and landing data cards just like any other aircraft and know if the air vehicle has achieved enough speed and distance to attempt take-off or abort, and enough distance if take-off is necessary for an immediate return to land.

or if ATC instructs the AVO to climb and maintain an altitude, the operator manually enters a heading and the required altitude. Another manual control is the command for flying a left or right 360° orbit at a specific altitude. If the AVO is told to keep the aircraft within a certain sector of airspace, the operator can enter go-to waypoints that are different to those in the mission plan. These ensure the aircraft stays within the new area while continuing to fly to the next planned way points, and if required at a different altitude.

If the control station loses the link, the aircraft has built in logic to autonomously recapture the mission plan and execute one of many different contingencies. These include flying itself back to its base or in the event of an emergency flying to a diversion field or to a ditch point where the aircraft will safely ditch away from areas of population. The contingencies are pre-programmed for emergency situations whenever the aircraft is on the mission plan route.

The AVO is responsible for making sure the aircraft is tied to the correct logic point for the real-time situation, however during the mission the operator can manually fly the aircraft using commanded airspeeds, altitudes,

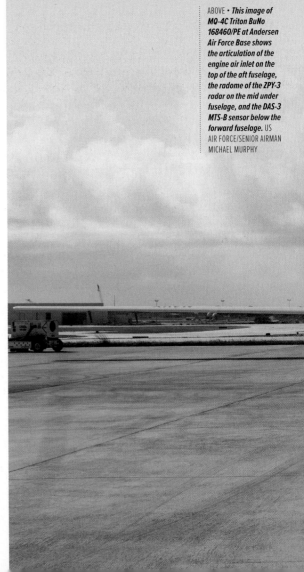

ABOVE • *This image of MQ-4C Triton BuNo 168460/PE at Andersen Air Force Base shows the articulation of the engine air inlet on the top of the aft fuselage, the radome of the ZPY-3 radar on the mid under fuselage, and the DAS-3 MTS-B sensor below the forward fuselage.* US AIR FORCE/SENIOR AIRMAN MICHAEL MURPHY

Mission plan areas are wide because the Triton flies so high for so long such that a request from the Carrier Strike Group commander to check a potential target of concern may already be covered by the mission plan area.

Logic to autonomously recapture the mission plan and execute one of many different contingencies is already built into the system, but the navy has a requirement to upload a new mission plan in flight. PMA-262 would not confirm if the latter capability is already integrated on MQ-4C air vehicles assigned to the fleet.

Recovery

When an aircraft is at the end of its on-station time and/or fuel load, and must return to base, the CONOPS is to replace it with another Triton which should arrive on station to provide continuous coverage of the area of operation. Once close to its FOB, the aircraft descends into the terminal area, and is handed over to the FOB AVO (although either control station can control the aircraft) and sets up for one of several approaches pre-programmed in the mission plan. Upon arrival at the initial approach fix the landing gear is lowered, and if not already done, the sensors are switched off. At the final approach fix the system switches to glide scope mode, and lines the aircraft up on the centre of the runway. On approach, the aircraft uses radio altimeters and four different navigation controls, two of which are for air vehicle navigation (the aircraft and its logic know it's geospatial location and its energy state) which control its approach flight with standard spoilers and engine throttle commands. When the system senses the runway, the aircraft flares, touches down, engages the brakes,

and stops on the runway centreline. If the system fails its own internal landing check, it waves itself off and climbs out and flies back into the pattern to make another approach to land. A wave off can also be manually selected by the AVO who can also manually fly the aircraft around the pattern for another autonomous approach to land.

Once the aircraft has stopped on the runway, the AVO selects the taxi command, and the aircraft autonomously taxies to the shutdown spot as programmed.

Integrated Functional Capabilities

In early 2020, PMA-262, the Persistent Maritime Unmanned Aircraft Systems Program Office based at Naval Air Station Patuxent River, Maryland reached a major milestone. Two MQ-4C Triton air vehicles configured with a software load named Integrated Functional Capability 3.2 (IFC 3.2, the operational baseline standard without a multi-intelligence capability), a launch and recovery, and maintenance teams were deployed to Andersen Air Force Base, Guam in support of the type's EOC (early operational capability). The navy defined the MQ-4C Triton's EOC requirement as having a main operating base and a forward operating base in operation, with two air vehicles at IFC 3 baseline configuration deployed outside of the continental United States.

At Patuxent River, PMA-262 continued to develop the next software load standard, IFC 4, which introduced an enhanced multi-intelligence sensor system as part of the US Navy's maritime intelligence, surveillance, reconnaissance and targeting transition plan.

headings, tracks, 360° patterns in both directions to prosecute a target, or find, identify, and follow a target of opportunity as needed.

Once a target of opportunity is done with, the AVO can command the aircraft to return to its programmed route or if the aircraft senses the AVO is no longer on the link, it autonomously returns to the mission plan and executes whatever contingency logic is appropriate for the situation.

BELOW • *A head-on shot shows the extent of the MQ-4C's 130ft 10in wingspan and the unusual cross-sectional shape of the forward fuselage.* US AIR FORCE/SENIOR AIRMAN MICHAEL MURPHY

169171

Developed and built by Northrop Grumman, the MQ-4C Triton is designed to acquire unprecedented situational awareness of the battle space to shorten the sensor-to-shooter decision loop in the maritime and littoral domains. The unmanned aerial system is also the first high altitude, long endurance aircraft that can conduct persistent intelligence, surveillance, and reconnaissance missions to complement the P-8A Poseidon in the maritime domain.

Milestone C and IFC 4

In conjunction with the MQ-4C Triton's Milestone C approval in September 2016, PMA-262 changed its acquisition strategy for the system by moving its initial operational test and evaluation (IOT&E) from Q4FY2017 to Q4FY2020 although though this did not happen. The change was made to align IOT&E with the development and fielding of IFC 4: the aircraft's all-important Multiple Intelligence (Multi-INT) capability and its full operational configuration.

The Multi-INT system provides Triton with an ELINT (electronic intelligence)

and SIGINT (signals intelligence) capability, and includes sensors, supporting software and hardware, which permit processing of classified sensitive compartmented information.

The Multi-INT configuration will augment the maritime ISR capability currently provided by the P-8A Poseidon and will ultimately replace the EP-3E Aries II intelligence gathering aircraft for most missions - one of the main objective roles of the Triton system.

PMA-262 conducted the first test flight of an MQ-4C Triton in the IFC4 configuration on July 29, 2021, at Naval Air Station Patuxent River, Maryland. PMA-262 said the functional check flight also involved initial aeromechanical test points, which demonstrated stability and control of the MQ-4C after a 30-month modification period.

At the time of the first flight, Captain Dan Mackin, Naval Air Systems Command's MQ-4C programme manager said the flight brought the MQ-4C Triton closer to achieving its initial operational capability (IOC) milestone.

In a September 14, 2023, news release, Northrop Grumman reported

the MQ-4C Triton had achieved a declaration of initial operating capability (IOC) by the US Navy. PMA-262 had not issued a press release on the IOC declaration by October 8, 2023.

The FY2024 US Navy's budget proposal outlines the service's intention to procure the final two MQ-4C aircraft for a total of 27 aircraft.

A May 2019 US Government Audit Office report found the projected Triton development costs had increased by 61% from $3.5bn in 2009 to nearly $5.7bn in October 2018. This is in part due to the navy's introduction of an advanced Multi-INT collection system to the programme of record; a major change to the system's requirements taken at the Triton Milestone C Baseline Requirements approval in September 2016. In addition, the program experienced challenges associated with SIGINT integration and realised the risk of the required rework to improve passive and active collection thresholds. Both factors increased the time required to successfully incorporate the Multi-INT capability and delayed its initial fielding by ~22

ABOVE • *An MQ-4C Triton unmanned aerial vehicle assigned to Unmanned Patrol Squadron 19 (VUP-19) at Naval Station Mayport, Florida, on October 14, 2022. VUP-19 is operating the MQ-4C to further develop the concept of operations and refine tactics, techniques, and procedures.* US NAVY/ MASS COMMUNICATION SPECIALIST AUSTIN COLLINS

RIGHT • *An MQ-4C Triton assigned to Unmanned Patrol Squadron 19 (VUP-19) takes off at Marine Corps Air Station Iwakuni, Japan, on October 5, 2022.* US MARINE CORPS/ LCPL DAVID GETZ

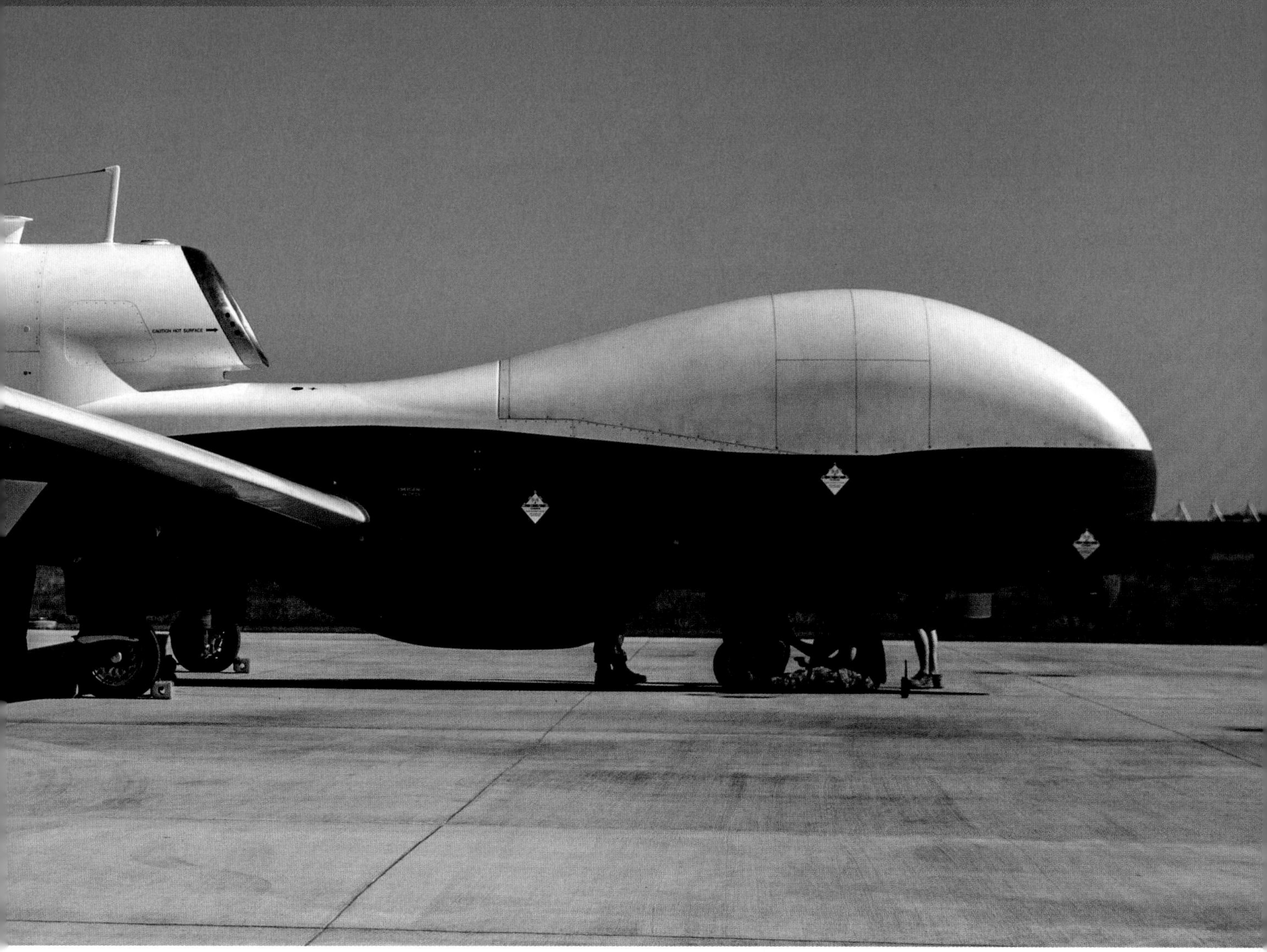
CAUTION HOT SURFACE

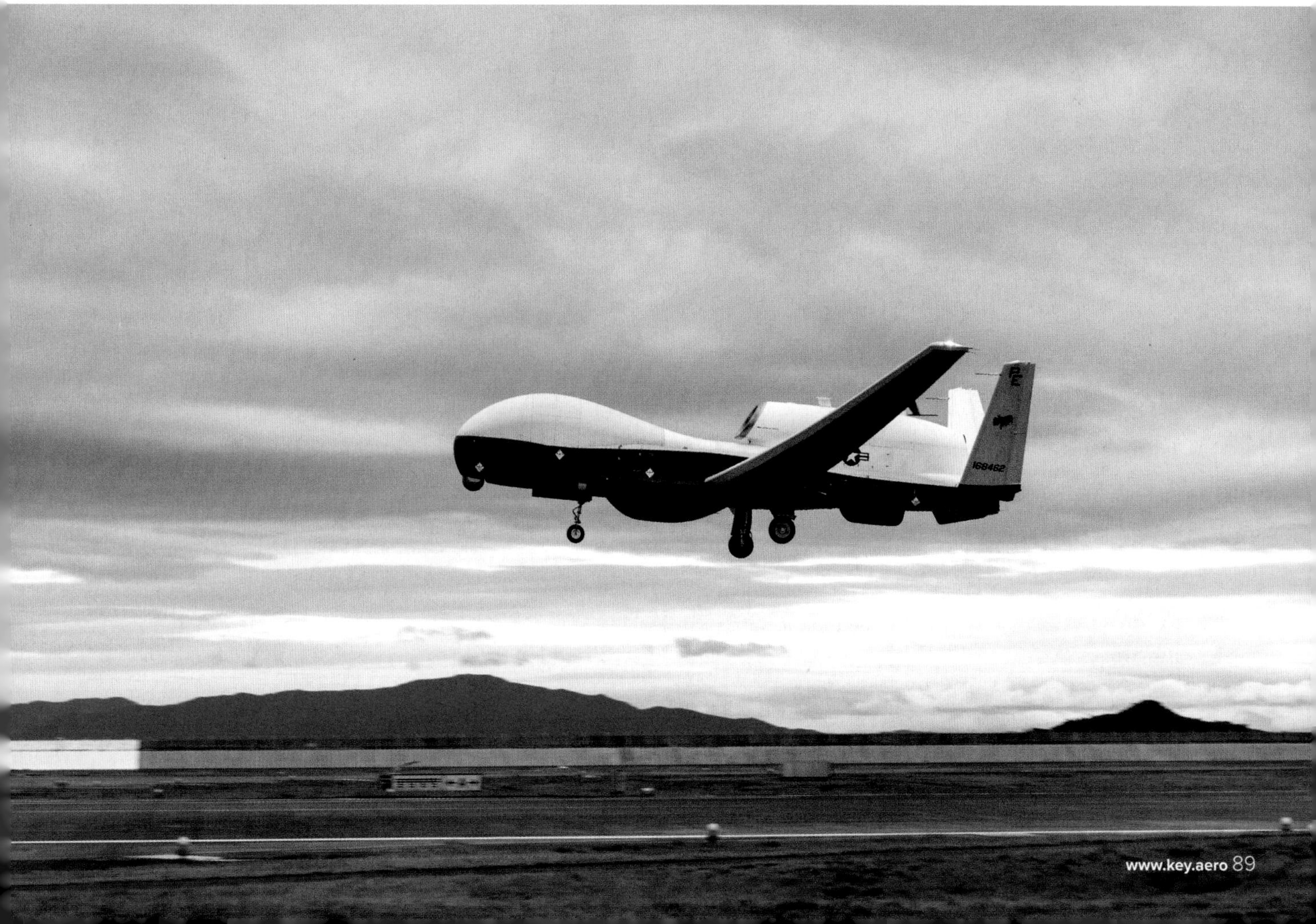
PE
168462

months. The MQ-4C programme has been refactored to deliver smaller increments of capability to flight test to reduce the risk of additional cost growth and delay.

In its June 2023 Weapons Systems Annual Assessment, the US Government Accountability Office said the MQ-4C Triton has no critical technologies. According to the MQ-4C programme, the IFC-4 design is stable; however, the US Navy continues to rework the MQ-4C cost and schedule baseline due in part to prior development delays.

According to the MQ-4C programme office, it began IFC-4 initial operational testing and evaluation, using a production representative prototype, in January 2023, with completion in April 2023, and planned to achieve IOC in August 2023, with two aircraft versus the previously planned four.

The programme is producing IFC-4 configured aircraft at the same time it is testing IFC-4. According to the programme office, the first IOC aircraft was delivered in October 2022, while the second IOC aircraft was on the production line at the time of the report, along with two others. The programme expected delivery of the three aircraft during the second and third quarters of FY2023.

EOC, VUP-19 and Guam Ops

In June 2019, PMA-262 and the ITT concluded an OA of the IFC 3 baseline configuration to support an early fielding decision of the MQ-4C Triton. According to the Director, Operational Test and Evaluation (DOT&E) FY2019 report, poor reliability, system immaturity, and adverse weather prevented PMA-262 and the ITT from completing the test in accordance with the DOT&E-approved test plan.

Five test flights were launched between July 2018 and May 2019, accruing 58.6 flight hours; the planned test was nine flights totalling 192 flight hours over three weeks. DOT&E published a classified OA report in December 2019.

DOT&E's 2019 assessment of the MQ-4C Triton said that suitability deficiencies related to reliability, documentation, training, and human-system interfaces interfered with the execution of the OA. The report also stated that the deficiencies also contributed to the loss of MQ-4C BuNo 168461 in a gear-up landing at Naval Air Station Point Mugu, California on September 12, 2018. The aircraft, assigned to VUP-19 experienced an inflight mechanical issue during a test

flight. As a precautionary measure, the AVOs shut down the engine and attempted to safely land the aircraft on the runway at Point Mugu. The aircraft's landing gear did not deploy, and the aircraft landed on the runway with its gear retracted.

MQ-4Cs used in the 2019 OA were configured with IFC 3.1, a standard that lacks the capability to disseminate maritime surface track data via Link 16 or the Global Command and Control System–Maritime. In September 2019, PMA-262 updated the air vehicle configuration to IFC 3.2 which provided the track data dissemination capability.

PMA-262 has also demonstrated a Due Regard Alternative Means of Compliance (DRAMOC) for the EOC, which alleviates, but does not eliminate, constraints on free navigation in the EOC area of operations. Naval Air Systems Command's Airworthiness Technical Authority certified the use of the Triton's sub-systems and NATOPS procedures to safely de-conflict from other aircraft with VUP-19 aircraft (employing the DRAMOC) during operations under due regard procedures in the 7th Fleet's area of responsibility. According to the DOT&E 2019 annual report, the DRAMOC is necessary because without it,

RIGHT • *An MQ-4C Triton unmanned aerial vehicle taxies at Marine Corp Air Station Iwakuni, Japan. Once the taxi command is given by the air vehicle operator, the aircraft taxies to the runway autonomously in accordance with the mission plan's route.* US MARINE CORPS/ CPL MITCHELL AUSTIN

BELOW • *An MQ-4C Triton assigned to Unmanned Patrol Squadron 19 (VUP-19), parked on the flight line at Naval Station Mayport, Florida.* US NAVY/ MASS COMMUNICATION SPECIALIST NATHAN BEARD

employment of the MQ-4C will be tightly constrained until delivery of the air traffic collision avoidance radar system estimated for FY2024.

The Triton programme office has also exercised the TCPED (tasking collection processing exploitation and dissemination) process which delivers real time information about targets within the air vehicle's 360° field of view to both forward deployed naval forces and the US national intelligence community.

At Andersen, VUP-19 is further developing a concept of operations and the fleet learning associated with operating a high-altitude, long-endurance system in the maritime domain. Back-end mission crew are operating from the squadron's facilities at Naval Air Station Jacksonville, Florida.

No doubt, some missions are being flown to directly support P-8A Poseidon maritime surveillance aircraft operating around the Pacific to increase the capabilities available from the two aircraft in a manned-unmanned teaming concept.

A Triton can track a surface target using its DAS-3 MTS-B camera and download full motion video to a P-8 crew positioned some distance away via a common datalink, thereby helping to build situational awareness of the battle space. In an operational scenario,

this capability enables the P-8 crew to familiarise itself with a target of interest and any surrounding vessels well in advance of the Poseidon's arrival on station.

Supporting this manned-unmanned teaming concept between an MQ-4C and a P-8A, the Triton force comprises aircrew who are nearly all second or third tour personnel from the Maritime Patrol and Reconnaissance Force. That means each one has completed multiple operational tours with either a P-3, P-8 or EP-3 squadron before they transition to Triton operations. This experience enables them to quickly learn the Triton mission and tactics, and better integrate with P-8 crews on station.

EOC is specifically designed to develop concepts for incorporating the MQ-4C into the maritime domain mission set to augment the navy's P-8A Poseidon and EP-3E Aries aircraft. Akin to a low earth orbiting satellite, the MQ-4C is a long-dwell system and a force multiplier within the family of aircraft flown by the US Navy's Maritime Patrol and Reconnaissance Force (MPRF). The MQ-4C is designed to provide cueing data to any of the MPRF aircraft types and identify vessels and areas of interest that manned aircraft can further investigate with their respective sensor suites.

VUP-19, in coordination with Patrol and Reconnaissance Wing 11 and the Pacific theatre commanders, established a multi-phase approach to EOC. The teamed organisations devised a series of metrics to measure sensor performance, crew familiarisation, and fleet integration, until a point when the commander of the Pacific Fleet was comfortable with declaring EOC based on the squadron's successful and effective performance on station. A culmination test was set in which an MQ-4C was tasked to conduct operations for a dynamic problem set and provide commanders with real-time intelligence.

Throughout the EOC deployment, Combined Task Force 72 and the 7th Fleet are using opportunities ranging from direct support missions, exercise involvement, and real-world ISR operations in theatre to develop the CONOPS and fleet learning associated with operating a high-altitude, long-endurance unmanned air vehicle in the maritime domain. More specifically, each mission and integration event with any US Navy or joint service asset deployed around the theatre provide ways for the fleet and joint services to understand and properly use Triton capabilities to meet the commander's requirements.

Intelligence Gatherers

Alexander Mladenov details Russia's electronic, signals and communication intelligence aircraft, the Ilyushin Il-20M Coot-A.

The Russian Air Force (Voenno-Vozdushnye Sily Rossii or VVS) fleet of about 15 Il-20M Coot-A ELINT/SIGNIT/COMINT aircraft is operated by numerous units, some of which have a single aircraft in their structures. For example, three or four are assigned to a unit at Kubinka near Moscow, subordinated to the 929th GLITs (Flight Test Centre); one aircraft is flying with the 610th TsBPiPLS (Combat Training and Aircrew Conversion Centre) of the MTA branch in Ivanovo-Severny, another is in the structure of the 30th OTSAP at Rostov-on-Don/Tsentralny, and the 257th OSAP (Independent Composite Aviation

Regiment) at Khabarovsk-Bolshoy has one more example. The Rostov on Don-based aircraft is tasked to perform missions in the Black Sea region and around the southern borders of Russia, while the aircraft from Kubinka operate over the Baltic and Barents Seas and the Il-20M from Khabarosk is used for intelligence-gathering over neutral waters in the Far Eastern region of Russia.

There are also aircraft in test and evaluation with the 929th GLITs and others are undergoing overhaul and upgrade at the 20 ARZ plant in Pushkin, near St Petersburg. There are also a few Il-20Ms held in long-term storage at Pushkin, to be used either as spare

parts donors or to be cycled through overhaul and upgrade.

The VVS Il-20M existing inventory, produced in the first half of the 1970s, is being life extended and receiving new mission suites. There were hints that small and large-scale upgrades applied to the Il-20M fleet over the years have resulted in unique mission suite configurations for each airframe in active service.

The Russian MoD's effort to boost the capabilities of the small strategic reconnaissance fleet has resulted in at least three comprehensive Il-20M upgrade standards introduced post 2000. The first two, known as Monitor and Anagramma, were introduced in the 2000s, adding new ELINT/SIGINT/

COMINT capability to bring the Il-20M into the digital era. The third one, known as Retsensent, added an even higher standard of ELINT/COMINT/SIGNINT equipment and electro-optical/infrared (EO/IR) sensors to deliver two more decades of service. The prototype Il-20M upgrade (known as Product 17MS) was developed under a contract between Ilyushin and the Russian MoD signed in February 2011, at a price of RUB 262.2m (approx $2.6m today), with completion of the state testing effort slated for the early 2020s.

The Retsensent prototype, retrofitted from one of the production-standard Il-20Ms, made its maiden flight in the spring of 2015 and had completed its factory testing phase by early 2018.

With the internal Ilyushin designation Izdeliye 17MS (Product 17MS), the highly-upgraded Il-20M retains the Il-20M's original large belly pod but housing a new-generation phased-array side-looking radar; and the large fairings on the forward fuselage have been reshaped, together with two pairs of large fairings behind the wings and on the rear fuselage. The belly also houses bulged fairings, believed to serve the newly-added ELINT, COMINT and SIGINT sensors, as well as an EO/IR sensor turret under nose. There are also arrays of newly-added antennas on the upper and lower fuselage and on the tail, associated with the highly-classified new mission suite.

Delayed retirement

The Il-20M fleet was originally due to be replaced by the jet-powered Tu-214R, equipped with a new-generation mission suite including a side-looking radar, EO, ELINT, SIGINT, COMINT and EO sensors. However, it now seems that both types are set to serve together, as the Tu-214R has proved to be a long-delayed and expensive programme, and no significant production run is believed to be planned. Two Tu-214Rs have been built so far, with the first flying for the first time in 2009, and both are currently in experimental operation with the VVS, Completion of their notably protracted testing effort slated for 2018, but as of October 2020 there were no reports that the plan had been met.

Russian Beepers and Squeakers

Alexander Mladenov outlines the Ilyushin Il-22PP Mute electronic warfare aircraft.

Developed under the Porubshchik programme (loosely translated 'Porubshchik' means chopper or axe), the Il-22PP is an airborne escort jammer and SIGINT aircraft, converted from the Il-22 airborne command post. It is equipped with a new-generation jammer suite to disrupt operations of airborne radars, land- and ship-based air defence radars, missile guidance radars, missile guidance radio command systems and tactical datalinks. This version is easily distinguished from the Il-22 thanks to two large fairings on either side of the fuselage, one in front of and one behind each wing. They house the antennae of the L-415 jammer suite developed by Kaluga-based KNIRTI company. The tail also sports a bulged fairing housing an unidentified antenna, the top of the fuselage has a receiver antenna fitted and a cigar-shaped antenna is installed under the mid-fuselage. The Il-22PP is also equipped with UV-26 chaff/flare dispensers installed in a pod under the fuselage for 26mm cartridges, plus two more dispenser units (for a total of 28 50mm rounds) in the rear fuselage.

Il-22PP development was launched by the Myasischev Company in 2009 and flight test of the prototype, wearing Russian pseudo-civil registration RA-75903, commenced in 2011. The testing effort was reportedly complete by 2015 and Myasischev subsequently completed a production batch of two further aircraft. These were handed over to the VVS in 2016 and 2017, respectively.

The three Il-22PPs (including the prototype upgraded to the production configuration) were delivered to the EW Detachment of the 117th VTAP, a front-line regiment of the VVS' Military Transport Command stationed at Orenburg, in 2017. The unit also operates three older-generation An-12PPS equipped for the EW role.

The popular website *The Aviationist* reported on the intercept of two VVS Il-22PP aircraft in international airspace near to the Baltic States on July 29, 2021. According to site: "The intercept mission was carried out by Spanish Air Force Eurofighters and Italian Air Force F-35s, both on Quick Reaction Alert duty in the Baltic region, which tracked, and intercepted the Russian aircraft en route to Russia from the Kaliningrad Oblast. It was the first time NATO aircraft had intercepted the Il-22PP in the region."

Swedish SIGINT

Mark Ayton details the Gulfstream IVSP-based S 102B Korpen operated by the Swedish Air Force – the Sverige Flygvapnet.

Prior to the final SIGINT mission flown by Sweden's TP85 Caravelle Fv85210 on November 19, 1998, a new type of jet was already in service conducting signal reconnaissance for Försvarets Radio Anstalt (FRA or the National Defence Radio Establishment) supporting the Swedish government's foreign, security and defence policy. That jet is the superlative Gulfstream IV SP-based S 102B Korpen. The Sverige Flygvapnet (Swedish Air Force) continues to operate two S 102Bs, Fv102002 'Huginn' and Fv102003 'Muninn' each named after a raven owned by the ancient Scandinavian god Odin. The type entered service with 73 SIGINT

Squadron based at Malmen Air Base in the autumn of 1997 and gained full mission capability during 1998. Both aircraft are managed by the Transport and Special Flights Unit, part of F 7 Skaraborg Wing based at Såtenäs Air Base.

Operated with a crew of six comprising a pilot, co-pilot and four system operators, S 102Bs are equipped for intercepting and recording both communication and electronic signals, COMINT and ELINT respectively, reportedly using an American SIGINT system built by Northrop Grumman and called the Wideband Tactical Surveillance System. The aircraft reportedly gathers COMINT information from transmissions in the 2MHz to 20GHz frequency range.

In comparison to its TP85 predecessor, and other western SIGINT aircraft such as the RC-135 Rivet Joint, the S 102B offers good endurance, higher airspeed (over 485kts) and altitude performance, which enables the aircraft to reach its tasked surveillance area faster, and when on station provide greater mission flexibility for intercepting technical signals transmitted by radars, navigation equipment and weapon systems. It achieves this level of performance despite an additional three tons of mission system payload compared to a baseline Gulfstream IV SP business jet.

Despite its Gulfstream IV SP baseline design, the S 102B is highly-modified. The SIGINT configuration features a large fairing fitted on either side of the forward fuselage, a canoe-style radome

BELOW • *S 102B Fv102003/023 parked on the flight line at Malmen Air Base.* FÖRSVARSMAKTEN

on the forward fuselage underside and a small blister on the nose. All three types of assembly house antennas or sensors. Like all SIGINT aircraft, the S 102B features an array of blade and hook antennas installed on the lower surfaces of the centre and aft fuselage, and wings.

The Korpen system includes high bandwidth, 2Mb/sec data links used to down link large volumes of data directly to the FRA's operations centres and Svenska Marinen (Royal Swedish Navy) ships and vessels.

Sweden's defence posture used to be participation in international military operations in a non-kinetic way. In the spring of 2018 and 2019, an S 102B deployed to RAF Akrotiri, Cyprus in support efforts by the western alliance to defeat the so-called Islamic State (ISIS) in Syria.

Operating from Cyprus, the Korpen was able to fly orbits in international air space to snoop on the latest Russian weapon systems operating in Syria (and those operated by the Assad regime) under combat conditions. Given Russia's deployment of Su-35 Flanker fighters, S-400 surface-to-air missiles and

Gravestone multi-mode engagement radars, the Korpen was perfectly placed to gather a swathe of new information on Putin's weapons of war, so highly valuable to the Swedish military machine. Information that allowed the Scandinavian nation to improve and optimise its own weapon systems as a means of countering potential new threats.

When operating from Malmen the two aircraft predominantly circuit over the Baltic Sea gathering COMINT and ELINT of Russian weapon systems operating from/to and in Kaliningrad. This enables the FRA to keep its intelligence databases up to date for use by the Swedish government, its intelligence agencies, and armed forces.

Changed circumstances

However, since Russia's unprovoked invasion of Ukraine in February 2022, Swedish S 102B aircraft have undertaken regular reconnaissance missions in Polish airspace along the border with Belarussia and Russia to snoop on military activity in each nation. Sweden is clearly integrating its S 102B operations in full cooperation

with US Air Forces in Europe and Air Forces Africa.

More recently, on August 2, 2023, a Swedish S 102B flew a reconnaissance mission for the first time in Finnish airspace close to the Kola Peninsula to gather intelligence on Russian weapon systems based in the region.

No doubt indicative of even greater cooperation between the two Nordic neighbours given their respective NATO membership status. Finland and Sweden completed NATO accession talks, and Allies signed the Accession Protocols for both countries in July 2022. Finland joined the Alliance on April 2, 2023, and Sweden is an official Invitee and attends NATO meetings as such. NATO Secretary General Jens Stoltenberg has highlighted that NATO's priority is for Sweden's accession to be completed as soon as possible.

According to the Swedish government's bill 'Totalförsvaret 2021–2025' (Total Defence 2021-2025) published in October 2020, both S 102B aircraft will be retained in service, with no planned replacement until after 2025.

Still in the Shadows

David Willis collates the data available on one of the RAF's most secretive assets, the Beechcraft Shadow.

The Shadow was procured to meet an Urgent Operational Requirement (UOR) issued in 2006 for a manned aerial surveillance aircraft to support British and coalition operations in Afghanistan. In July 2007, four Beech 350CER King Airs were ordered as part of a contract with Raytheon Systems Ltd (RSL). The King Air family was already a popular special missions' platform – with around 50 different configurations – offering a satisfactory combination of performance, internal space, and operating costs, while it had a lower profile than 'pure' military types, thanks to its widespread use as a corporate transport. The 350CER is equipped with a 'cargo' door ('C') and additional fuel tanks aft of the engine nacelles to give extended range ('ER'). It is certified as a version of the Model B300C with optional packages, the 350-designation existing strictly for marketing purposes.

Only for the Duration

It was originally rumoured that the King Airs were destined for the Army Air Corps, to augment or replace the Britten-Norman Islanders and Defenders, and it was confirmed only in December 2008 that the aircraft would be operated by the RAF as ISTAR platforms, known as Shadow R1s.

Airframe modifications would be performed by GAMA Support Services at Farnborough, Hampshire, and the mission systems installed by Raytheon at Hawarden outside Chester. Beech 350CER G-JENC (c/n FM-14) arrived at Hawarden for completion on October 14, 2007, departing in November 2008 for Norwich Airport to be painted in the light grey scheme applied to the fleet. The following month it was at RAF Waddington, Lincolnshire, for trials and crew training. It joined No.5 (Army Co-operation) Squadron on May 27, 2009, as ZZ416, its civil registration having been cancelled the same day.

The squadron had operated the five Sentinel R1 Airborne Stand-Off Radar (ASTOR) platforms since they entered service in December 2008, but formed Shadow Flight to fly its new equipment. The Shadow entered operational service in July 2009, with ZZ416 joined by ZZ417 (c/n FM-16, ex G-NICY) on July 27, ZZ418 (c/n FM-17, ex G-JIMG) on September 4, and ZZ419 (c/n FM-18, ex G-OTCS) on December 10.

On October 14, 2011, No.14 Squadron reformed and received the assets of Shadow Flight. A fifth Shadow R1 (ZZ504, c/n FM-48) arrived at RAF Waddington on December 12, 2011. It was initially delivered as a Beech 350CER to GAMA Support Services at Farnborough on April 30, 2011, before going to Hawarden by May 12 for installation of its mission systems. Military markings were applied on December 9, the day its previous identity (G-CGUM) was cancelled. Initially the squadron used the new Shadow as a crew trainer for the four aircraft already in service.

As originally planned it was expected that the Shadow would have a short career, like all equipment procured

BELOW • *The extensive modifications made to the King Air airframe to create the Shadow include an under-fuselage pannier with an electro-optical sensor, plus two large ventral strakes under the rear fuselage.*
DAVID WILLIS

under UORs. This was confirmed in the 2010 Strategic Defence and Security Review (SDSR), when it was announced they would be withdrawn at the end of UK combat operations in Afghanistan.

Systems and Operations

Significant modifications were undertaken on the King Airs to create the Shadows. The most prominent was a large under fuselage pannier with an electro-optical/infrared sensor at the rear, stated by Raytheon to be a L-3 Wescam MX-15. A total of 21 mission systems were installed in the Shadow R1. Raytheon lists 'integrated intelligence-gathering sensor systems', line-of-sight and satcom datalinks, and a 360° self-protection suite among the equipment carried. Other sources list a forward looking, wide-area surveillance sensor for the counter-improvised explosive device (C-IED) role, a Raytheon Airborne Vision Enhanced System (AVES), and HF, UHF and VHF radios. The aircraft was configured to relay data to troops on the ground equipped with a ROVER (Remotely Operated Video Enhanced Receiver) terminal. It has a flight crew of two and three operator workstations within the cabin, while another two mission personnel can also be accommodated.

One item that had not been noted on the Shadow are wing hardpoints. However, intriguingly, the EASA Type Certificate notes that the first five aircraft would require "re-evaluation of structure and fatigue... prior to import back into the United States" because of the addition of wing hard points (known as MOD007710). This stipulation does not appear to apply to later conversions.

The exact role of the Shadow – described by the RAF as 'offensive support' – has never been elucidated by the Ministry of Defence, beyond the fact it was acquired for service over Afghanistan. Until the arrival of the Shadow in theatre (and the similar MC-12W Liberty Bell flown by the US Air Force) ISTAR support to special forces was provided by General Atomics MQ-1 Predator and MQ-9 Reaper unmanned air vehicles (UAV), and US Navy Lockheed P-3 Orion and RAF Nimrod MR2 maritime patrol aircraft (MPA). While the UAVs excelled at providing persistent live coverage, their operators were far away from the battlefield and lacked the 'ground truth' understanding of the tactical situation vital to operations. Extensive communication facilities, plus room to include members of the special forces among the mission crews, made MPAs useful intelligence assets, but they were short on endurance and had limited sensor capability. Both UAVs and MPAs were manpower intensive and expensive to operate.

The Shadow combined the best aspects of both in a single platform, while benefiting from lower costs and a smaller support footprint. The first deployment was undertaken in December 2009 by ZZ419, which operated from Kandahar airfield in the south of Afghanistan. Arrival of the aircraft in theatre allowed the Nimrod to be replaced and withdrawn in April 2010.

Very little has ever been revealed about the operations undertaken, partly because the aircraft regularly supported special forces, about which the British government refuses to comment. A report on the RAF Waddington website in August 2012 stated that the Shadow had been "permanently patrolling the skies above Afghanistan since 2009, gathering vital intelligence on insurgent activities." The Shadow

LEFT • *Top view of Shadow R1 ZZ504, showing the 'saddle' tanks aft of the engine nacelles.* CPL STEVE BUCKLEY/CROWN COPYRIGHT

would gather real time information over wide areas. This could include recording 'pattern of life' information, allowing the hideouts of those planting IEDs to be identified by 'rewinding' recorded footage, or monitoring areas through which patrols travelled. Using its sensors, the Shadow can provide tactical support to troops (usually special forces) on the ground, providing an overview of the situation, relaying the information direct to the screens of ROVER terminals carried

by the soldiers. The fleet recorded its 10,000th operational flight hour over Afghanistan on July 19, 2012.

Beechcraft Shadows continued to deploy overseas even after the 2020-2021 withdrawal from Afghanistan, indicating use in other theatres. The type has been used to support Operation Shader, the codename for British military invention against the so-called Islamic State (ISIS). British special forces have reportedly operated in Iraq, Syria, Libya, and Tunisia as part

of Shader, and it is likely the Shadow supported them.

Core Equipment

Delivery of a sixth Shadow was revealed by Dr Andrew Murrison, the Minister for International Security Strategy on July 4, 2013. The announcement was also the first indication that the Shadow had a career post-Afghanistan, as it would be brought into the core RAF fleet, effectively making the service responsible for its continued funding

BELOW • *As part of the upgrade programme the Shadow R1+ received a large bulge on the top of the fin which is believed to accommodate a satellite communications antenna.* DAVID WILLIS

ABOVE • *Shadow R1+ ZZ418 lines up on the runway at RAF Waddington in November 2021 at the start of a training flight.*
DAVID WILLIS

rather than out of the separate budget for UORs. This was confirmed during a speech by Chief of the Air Staff Air Chief Marshal Sir Andrew Pulford at DESi in London on September 10, 2013.

The sixth aircraft was Beech 350CER G-LBSB (c/n FM-55) with a 'slick' interior, which arrived at RAF Waddington from Hawarden on June 30, 2013. It was delivered to GAMA at Farnborough on July 15 and departed back to Hawarden the same day.

Commitments under the 2015 SDSR released that November included growing the core funded fleet from five to eight aircraft. It involved conversion of the flight trainer (G-LBSB) operated by GAMA with a roll-on/roll-off mission system, plus two new airframes. The new airframes were both Beech 350Cs, without the nacelle 'saddle' tanks of the 'ER' variants. The first was G-GMAD (c/n FM-54), built as N51154 and delivered to GAMA in 2013, which adopted its British civil registration on September 27 that year. The second (N6029S, c/n FM-29) was a 2009-vintage aircraft that had previously served with the Saudi Arabia Presidency of Meteorology & Environment, before going to Avmet International and Tenax Aerospace in 2013. It was registered G-DAYP with GAMA on October 19, 2017.

Given the low profile of the Shadow, it was somewhat surprising that the aircraft featured in the flypast over The Mall in London to mark the 100th anniversary of the formation of the RAF. Two Shadows were among the aircraft that flew over Buckingham Palace on July 10, 2018, the first public appearance by the type. A few days later the Team Shadow agreement was

revealed, bringing the RAF, Raytheon UK, and Textron Aviation together with the aim of improving the effectiveness of both the Sentinel and Shadow fleets. One of the successes of Team Shadow, according to the Assistant Chief of Staff for Command, Control, Intelligence, Surveillance and Reconnaissance, Air Commodore Ian Gale, speaking at Farnborough 2018, was to cut implementation of the Shadow upgrade programme "from about five years to 18 months."

Upgrade Plans

Plans to upgrade the fleet were revealed in SDSR 2015. A two-phase programme was initiated, involving the aircraft becoming interim Shadow R1+s (although R1A has also been used) and then R2s. According to Raytheon, changes introduced in the R1+ were centred upon 'modularity and connectivity' improvements to

support the R2 configuration. External differences included the addition of a 'bulge' antenna at the top of the fin.

The first R1+ was ZZ417, which was returned to No.14 Squadron and departed overseas on March 9, 2018. At that point, the fleet based at RAF Waddington also included R1s ZZ416, ZZ418, ZZ419, and ZZ504, while 350Cs G-DAYP and G-GMAD had yet to be modified. Raytheon was working on G-LBSB at Hawarden, which would emerge as R1+ ZZ507 on May 16, 2018. The initial operational capability of the R1+ was due at the end of 2019.

The Shadow R2 upgrade aimed to create a network connected aeroplane with readily upgradeable system architecture, to keep pace with adversaries on the ground. New sensors and communications equipment were planned with greater use made of software automation to reduce workload.

RIGHT • *The pannier contains multiple sensors, including the optics for the wide area surveillance system as well as the electro-optical 'ball' for investigating specific targets.*
DAVID WILLIS

A Shadow Long-term Sustainment contract was awarded to RSL in 2019 by the Defence Equipment & Support's Fixed-Wing Manned Airborne Surveillance Delivery Team. The 11 year £250m deal, which came into effect from April 2019, supports operations and, according to ISTAR Programme Director Group Captain Shaun Gee, "enables future, rapid development of

the Shadow platform, which will ensure the capability remains at the cutting edge of technology, providing a world-class tactical intelligence surveillance reconnaissance capability for the UK."

An expansion to the programme was announced on November 3, 2021. The £110m awarded to Raytheon UK included funds to bring the fleet up to eight aircraft, plus new self-protection systems under

the Next Generation Air Survivability programme run by Team Pellonia. From 2022 the fleet was to be fitted with the Leonardo-Thales Miysis directed-infrared countermeasure defensive aids system, Thales Elix-IR threat warner and Thales Vicon XF countermeasures dispensing system, all part of Leonardo's Modular Advanced Platform Protection System.

The seventh and eight aircraft became the first Shadow R2s. They became ZZ505 (ex G-DAYP) and ZZ506 (ex G-MAD) after their civil registrations were cancelled on July 4 and April 8, 2022. On March 9, 2023, the final critical design review was passed, confirming the baseline configuration for the R2, and defining its equipment fit, with the initial delivery to the RAF scheduled for June 2023 (but not reported by October that year). It was planned that the Shadow R2 would enter service in 2024 and all upgrade aircraft would be (re)delivered before the end of 2025. No.14 Squadron is expected to operate the fleet until 2030, the current out-of-service date for the aircraft. It is likely that the full story of the Shadow will only emerge at some point after that date...

ABOVE • *The Shadow made its public debut during the flypast in July 2018 over London. Here an R1+ leads an R1 over RAF Cranwell on July 3, 2018, during the practice for the event.* GORDON ELIAS/ CROWN COPYRIGHT

LEFT • *While Shadows can be watched operating at RAF Waddington, little of what the aircraft does, or its exact configuration has entered the public domain.* DAVID WILLIS

The Fall and Rise of COCO ISR

Operations in Afghanistan and Iraq at the start of the 21st century meant an urgent need for ISR assets. David Willis looks at the changing demands for contractor-owned/contractor-operated (COCO) platforms.

One of the consequences of the Middle East conflicts at the beginning of the century was an urgent need for intelligence, surveillance, and reconnaissance (ISR) assets. This demand resulted in many different contractor-owned/contractor-operated (COCO) platforms being used to meet the growing demand for surveillance. Many disappeared quickly with the drawdown in operations. However, many were integrated within the US Army's wider ISR plans and recently there has been a resurgence in army demand for COCO operations.

Prior to the 9/11 attacks, the US Army planned to have 47 Beech RC-12 Guardrail aircraft and eight de Havilland Canada EO-5 Airborne Reconnaissance Lows (ARL) in operation. However, at the height of operations in Afghanistan and Iraq, their special mission fixed wing ISR fleet had increased to 110 platforms of many different kinds (some deployed in ones or twos) with multiple capabilities, many procured via Overseas Contingency Operation funds. They included aircraft purchased or modified, as well as COCO or government-owned/contractor-operated (GOCO) assets.

US Army Plans

The US Army's ISR fleet has undergone significant changes in the last few years. By the time it withdrew from combat operations it envisaged a manned fixed-wing fleet of nine ARLs - although using the twin-turboprop Bombardier (de Havilland Canada) DHC-8 Series 300 airframe rather than the four-engine Dash 7 of the EO-5C - 14 RC-12X Guardrail Common Sensors, 24 Mission Configurable Multi-Intelligence aircraft based on the Beech 350ER King Air, and four existing Quick Reaction Capability (QRC) wartime contingency aircraft. This was expected to be achieved around 2017. It also saw the service bring many ISR activities 'back in house' after widespread use of contractor assets and services to meet urgent operational requirements in the Middle East and South Asia.

Plans to transition from the EO-5C Airborne Reconnaissance Low-Multifunction (ARL-M) to the RO-6A Airborne Reconnaissance Low-Enhanced (ARL-E) that used the twin turboprop DHC-8 'Dash 8' Series 300 had been released by the US Army in 1994. The RO-6As were created by converting contractor-operated Dash 8s in several other ISR configurations,

including Saturn Arch and Desert Owl II, to a new common standard.

Saturn Arch began in 2010 as an airborne geospatial intelligence programme aimed at neutralising improvised explosive devices (IED) in Afghanistan. It was initially run by the National Geospatial-Intelligence Agency and was in service by 2012, using several different platforms.

Saturn Arch aircraft carried the Raytheon ACES Hy (Airborne Cueing and Exploitation System-Hyperspectral) and OG Systems PeARL (Performance-Enhanced Airborne Reconnaissance Low) wide-area sensor, General Atomics CLAW (a Windows-based integrated sensor payload control and analysis software package) plus two other systems known as Big Green. Big Green had been developed by the Lawrence Livermore National Laboratory, and the Mission Sensor System. The Saturn Arch programme was handed over to US Army Intelligence and Security Command (INSCOM) at a ceremony held at Kandahar airport on March 1, 2013, although the transition of elements from the 513th Military Intelligence Brigade, the US Army Geospatial Intelligence Battalion, and Task Force ODIN-E (Observe, Detect, Identify, and

BELOW • The Dash 8 Series 300 was used in both Saturn Arch and Desert Owl II configurations produced by Dynamic Aviation and SAIC, as well as forming the basis for the subsequent RO-6A Airborne Reconnaissance Low-Enhanced platforms.
US ARMY

Neutralize – Enhanced) had begun several months earlier.

The original Desert Owl was an airborne intelligence, surveillance, and reconnaissance system able to simultaneously conduct measurement and signature intelligence (MASINT) and imagery intelligence (IMINT) missions in nearly all weather conditions. It was a COCO Beech A200T King Air equipped with a PenRad 7 long-range, ultra-high frequency, synthetic-aperture radar array L-3 MX-15 electro-optical/infra-red sensor, able to identify changes on the ground over time to help counter IEDs and use a laser illuminator and designator for precision targeting. SRI International of Menlo Park, California, was awarded a contract for Desert Owl II on August 28, 2008. It was originally a 90-day deployment by a PenRad 7-equipped King Air to Iraq. Desert Owl operations later passed to Dynamic Aviation and the system eventually transitioned to a Dash 8.

The Dynamic Dash 8

The Dynamic Aviation Group of Bridgewater Air Park, Virginia, describes itself as 'the leading provider of modified aircraft, leased and operated worldwide in niche markets'. Provision of ISR has been a key part of its business since 2004, when it won a contract for a King Air 200 ISR sensor modification package. It currently has more than 140 aircraft and its customers include US defence, military intelligence, and other federal agencies; state and local governments; research organisations; and private companies.

In addition to King Airs, at least 41 Dash 8s have been registered to

LEFT • *DHC-8-202 N8200H was acquired by Dynamic Aviation from Vision Air in October 2009 as N801VA and operated on behalf of the US Army. The 'sidecars' along the fuselage contained sensors, while a satellite communications antenna was mounted in the radome on upper forward fuselage.* MARK HARKIN

BELOW • *Beech C-12C King Air N46L owned by Dynamic Aviation at North Los Vegas Airport in February 2011 with a CAESAR pod under the fuselage. The aircraft originally served with the US Army as 77-22945 before going to the Alaskan Government as N771AK before being sold to Dynamic in 2006.* TOMÁS DEL CORO

Dynamic Aviation, with the first acquired around 2009. It has operated Series 100s (14 airframes identified) and 200s (ten) with the original length fuselage, plus some 17 of the stretched Series 300 variant. Many of these aircraft were modified for ISR missions.

Its first was a Series 100 (N1000, c/n 024) acquired for a contract funded by the Joint IED Defeat Organization (JIEDDO) for operation within US Central Command's (USCENTCOM) area of responsibility under the Radiant Falcon programme. The aircraft was equipped with a L-3 Wescam MX-20SW short wave hyperspectral imager and control/exploitation system, optimised for area/spot measurement and signature intelligence in a sponson on the left-hand side of the aircraft. A standard MX-20 electro-optical sensor was installed under the fuselage. A pannier

under the centre fuselage contained a UHF synthetic aperture radar (SAR), with a geolocation device in another under the rear of the aircraft (removed by 2012), while a Ku-band SAR created by Sandia National Labs was installed in an extended nose. The Technology and Advanced Solution division of SAIC (now Leidos) was the lead systems contractor.

The aircraft was deployed to Bagram in Afghanistan from around 2011 under a COCO contract fulfilled by SAIC and Dynamic. During a night stop at Norwich Airport in the UK on November 29, 2012, it was seen to have nine cartoon bomb mission markings on the nose, including two with lit fuses and crossed-out eyes! The aircraft was re-registered N8100V by 2013 and is understood to have ended operations around 2014. Its mission systems had been removed no later than mid-2016.

Dynamic's Series 300s were equipped for the Saturn Arch (10 aircraft) and Desert Owl II (two) roles and operated under contract for the US Army. Both configurations were externally similar, with a large radome on the forward fuselage for satellite communication, light grey undersides with a darker shade on the upper surfaces, US Army titles on the tail, and civil registrations. Sensors were contained within large panniers (known as 'sidecars') along the lower side of the fuselage below the wing.

Both configurations provided persistent surveillance in both Afghanistan and Iraq to establish 'patterns of life' and counter IEDs. They could trace insurgent movements back to bomb workshops or safe houses, helping US forces to identify and locate suspects.

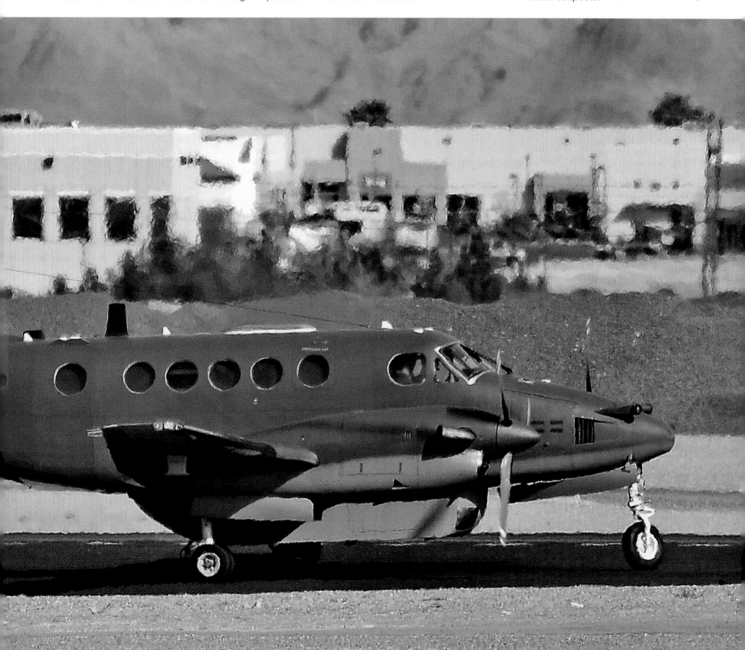

In 2015 it was planned that the Saturn Arch aircraft would be upgraded as RO-6As, and the quick reaction capability would end in FY2017. The QRC did remain active beyond this date, however, with three Dash 8s noted at Camp Humphreys in South Korea and one at Fort Bliss, Texas in July 2017. In October 2020, Leidos received a contract to sustain the programme, while one aircraft was noted operating over Libya in early 2021.

In August 2022 it was announced that on July 31 the Saturn Arch aircraft had completed their last mission in support of USCENTCOM. Over 10 years the aircraft had flown 72,500 hours and produced more than 18,000 intelligence products (although it was not confirmed if these figures related to just USCENTCOM operations or the programme as a whole).

Enhanced ARL

The US Army wanted nine RO-6A ARL-Es, including one as a trainer. A sources sought/request for information document released by the service in July 2013 included the need for a contractor to deliver the capability for up to five years in Afghanistan, South Korea, in the United States and other 'then yet-to-be-determined' locations. Leidos was tasked with delivering ARL-E, in partnership with the Sierra Nevada Corporation (SNC) and received a US$661.8m contract in November 2015 that was expected to be concluded five years later.

The RO-6A would be equipped with the Northrop Grumman AN/ZPY-5 VADER (Vehicle and Dismount Exploitation Radar) and ground moving target indication/SAR Long Range Radar, a L-3 Wescam MX-20D short-range infrared and MX-20HD electro-optical/infrared sensors, the Raytheon ACES Hy and OG Systems PeARL 5.0, L-3 intercommunications and beyond line-of-sight datalinks, and an Argon ST communication intelligence system. The latter comprising the PRISM 2.X/EDM-B, Banshee II HF and VHF, and Gen 5 Adder, plus

BELOW • *MARSS-equipped DHC-7-102 Dash 7 N176RA shortly after arriving at Davis-Monthan AFB, Arizona, in August 2016 after being withdrawn. The aircraft reportedly had flush covers covering optical instruments to hide some of its capabilities while on the ground.*

Digital Receiver Technology's DRT1201C and DRT2183C, for signal emitter geolocation. The sensors were controlled and operated using six Distributed Common Ground Station-Army (DCGS-A) compliant multifunction workstations in the cabin.

On April 7, 2015, the US Army announced it would acquire six Dash 8 Series 300 airframes from the Dynamic Aviation Group under a US$39.2m deal. Most, if not all, were already configured for Saturn Arch or Desert Owl II and had previously operated under contract to the US Department of Defense. The civil registrations of all six were cancelled in mid-November 2015 or early January 2016 and they were allocated US Army

serials 15-10332, 15-10338, 15-10348, 15-10352, 15-10358 and 15-10577, the last three digits duplicating the aircraft's constructor's number. Four of the RO-6As would be configured from Saturn Arch aircraft, one (15-10577) from Desert Owl II, while 15-10348 was understood to be the trainer.

Dynamic Aviation also acquired another four Dash 8 Series 300s for supply to the US Army as RO-6As. Two had previously flown with DAC Aviation East Africa of Kenya and were registered to Dynamic as N308V (c/n 397) and N308H (c/n 374) in September 2016 and August 2017, before becoming 16-00397 and 16-00374. Also in August 2017, VH-QQN (c/n 276) of Air Fleet

Management briefly became N308N then 16-00276 that November. The fourth was N590K (c/n 590), previously PK-TUB of Travita Air, which was registered to Dynamic between August 2018 and December 2021. It became 16-00590 in August 2020.

This gave the US Army ten airframes for the ARL-E programme, one more than originally sought. The April 2013 budget request justification document for ARL-E stated the series aircraft would be acquired during FY2015 (four), FY2016 (two), FY2017 (two) and FY2018 (one), with 16-00590 falling outside this scheme.

Plans for the US Army's ISR fleet, however, had changed.

ABOVE • *TACOP LIDAR Beech 350 N6461F on approach to RAF Mildenhall, a frequent stop over for QRC aircraft transiting to and from the Middle East. The aircraft had become 11-00283 and was later converted as a MC-12S EMARSS.* KEY PUBLISHING

On March 30, 2022, its Program Executive Office for Aviation confirmed the service was in the process of divesting itself of the RO-6As. Except for one retained for test duties, all the aircraft were out of service by October 2022, with most stored at Salina Regional Airport in Kansas. The remaining RO-6A (former Desert Owl II 15-00277) is assigned to the Communications-Electronics Research, Development and Engineering Center's (CERDEC) Flight Activity of the Intelligence Information Warfare Directorate (I2WD) based at Joint Base McGuire-Dix-Lakehurst, New Jersey.

Two of the last four RO-6As acquired were registered to the US Department of Homeland Security (DHS) in 2023, with 16-00374 becoming N804MR on March 14 and 16-00590 N810MR on May 30. DHS has around eight other Dash 8s, most equipped with the SeaVue maritime radar and an EO/IR sensor. It has not been confirmed in what configuration the two new additions to the DHS fleet will be operated.

Where Did the GOCO King Airs Go?

The requirement for 24 Mission Configurable Multi-Intelligence aircraft was met by the Boeing MC-12S Enhanced Medium Altitude Reconnaissance and Surveillance System (EMARSS), an ISR variant of the Beech 350 King Air. Plans to acquire additional new build EMARSSs were replaced in June 2015 by the EMARSS Follow-on Variant Modification (EMARSS-FVM) programme, involving the conversion of a mix of former US Air Force MC-12W Liberty turboprops and QRC King Airs instead.

The QRC King Airs involved comprised five in Constant Hawk – Afghanistan configuration, three Tactical Operations – Light Detection and Ranging (TACOP LIDAR) aircraft, and four Medium Altitude Reconnaissance and Surveillance Systems (MARSS). These aircraft were all government-owned but contractor-operated (GOCO). Five pre-owned Beech 350s had been equipped as C-IED surveillance platforms under the Constant Hawk-Afghanistan programme. L-3 Communications was awarded a contract in February 2009 to supply and operate four in Afghanistan, while the fifth was to remain in the United States to continue systems development. The aircraft had a ventral pannier that contained electro-optical sensors and were equipped with a satcom and real-time data link, while the BAE Systems Airborne Wide Area Persistent Surveillance System was due to be fielded on the aircraft from the third quarter of FY2010. In 2016 they became 11-00282 (ex N316W) and 12-00278 to 12-00281

(ex N15EW, N6116N, N6179X/N73WW and N45J, respectively).

The TACOP LIDAR (light detection and ranging) aircraft carried sensors to detect subtle changes on the surface of the ground to reveal recently buried items, such as IEDs. Two Beech 350is were ordered by the US Air Force in December 2010 on behalf of the US Army and in March 2011, L-3 was awarded a contract to modify them to the TACOP LIDAR configuration within 12 months. A third was soon added to the programme, with all three with L-3 by July 2011. N6461F had adopted the military serial 11-00283 by April 2014, and N8107F and N8148S became 11-00284 and 11-00285 in late 2016.

A total of 20 aircraft of three types were equipped with MARSS, sometimes known as the Multi-Sensor Airborne (rather than Medium Altitude) Reconnaissance and Surveillance System. It used a L-3 MX-15i with full motion video (FMV) imaging and SIGINT equipment to detect, identify, and report threat targets in near real-time. Equipment installed changed over the length of the programme, with some aircraft being equipped with the VADER radar to detect mobile targets.

The first MARSS was deployed in the US Southern Command area of operations in the early 2000s. Additional systems were fielded for use initially in Afghanistan, although they later also operated in Iraq. They were also used on peacekeeping duties on behalf of US European Command following the violent break-up of Yugoslavia.

By June 2011, MARSS had been installed in 11 Beech 300 King Airs and was also in a pair of Beech 200 King Airs and two Dash 7s. The DHC-7-102s (at least) were government-owned and contractor-operated. They were retired to Davis-Monthan Air Force Base in Arizona for storage with the 309th Aerospace Maintenance and Regeneration Group on August 29, 2016 (N176RA, c/n 76) and August 8, 2017 (N566CC, c/n 56). They had operated out of Kandahar in 2011 and at least one was

noted over Benghazi in April 2016, and Derna to the east of the Libyan city in January 2017.

Until early 2021, seven MARSS King Airs were assigned to INSCOM within USCENTCOM. Their withdrawal left three 2009-vintage Beech 300s operated for US Special Operations Command within the region, the final MARSS in service. They ended operations on September 30, 2021, and were flown back to the United States to have their mission systems removed. During their time in the Middle East, they flew an average of 90 missions a month, recording over 130,000 flight hours. They were officially retired in March 2022.

While eight MC-12Ws would become MC-12S-2 EMARSS-Ms (Multi-Intelligence), the Constant Hawk and TACOP LIDAR aircraft were designated MC-12S-1 EMARSS-Gs (Geo Intelligence) and MARSS became MC-12S-3 or S-4 (11-00287 only) EMARSS-Vs (VADER). (The MC-12S-4 may be a former MARSS aircraft not equipped with VADER.) The converted aircraft augmented four airframes procured for the EMARSS engineering and manufacturing demonstration phase, later becoming MC-12S EMARSS-S (Signals), to give a total of 24 aircraft.

From the late 2010s the US Army began to investigate the composition of its future ISR fleet. As focus turned away from counter terrorist activities toward peer and near-peer adversaries (with an increasing shift of emphasis towards the Indo-Pacific region – particularly China) senior leadership in the US Army's ISR hierarchy began to express a need to invest in new capabilities and platforms. It meant a move away from operations in permissive airspace to potentially contested airspace, with operations at higher altitude to increase the area that could be covered by the platform's sensors. They wanted greater emphasis on speed and range to assure access to areas without having to rely on allied military installations to undertake missions and reduce the vulnerability of its ISR assets in times of tension.

These challenges resulted in the creation of an ISR Task Force and the High-Accuracy Detection and Exploitation System (HADES) programme of record, the airborne component of the new overarching Multi-Domain Sensing System (MDSS). It also meant investment in Aerial Technology Demonstrators (ATD) to develop concepts of operation, new sensors, and test platforms, with large cabin business jets seen as the preferred solution. In an era of tightening budgets, the decision was taken to contract out the ATDs and their operation. The first was ARTEMIS.

COCO Demonstrators

The Airborne Reconnaissance Targeting Exploitation Mission Intelligence System (ARTEMIS) was launched in May 2019 to demonstrate improved COMINT, ELINT and geolocations capabilities as part of the wider HADES programme. A pair of Bombardier CL-600-2B16 Challengers, owned and operated by Leidos, have been modified as ARTEMIS testbeds and are based at Manassas Regional Airport in Virginia.

The first was Challenger 650 N488CR (c/n 6140) registered to Lasai Aviation of Virginia. It has a low pannier housing sensors under the front fuselage and extending under the wing centre section, strakes under the rear fuselage, and multiple aerials above and below the cabin. Challenger 604 N9191 (c/n 5312 ex N312AM), registered to Tenax Aerospace of Mississippi, is the second aircraft. It has a different sensor configuration, with a radome under the front fuselage that does not disrupt airflow to the extent it requires ventral strakes.

Soon after completing aircraft and sensor system engineering, airworthiness qualification, information assurance accreditation, integration, and test requirements, both aircraft deployed to Kadena Air Base, Okinawa in July

2020 to fly missions for US Indo-Pacific Command. This was before the ATD had been officially revealed by the US Army's Program Executive Office on August 6. The following month the first aircraft was in Europe, flying from Mihail Kogălniceanu Airport in southeast Romania in the Black Sea region, including over Georgia during Exercise Noble Partner 20 held in conjunction with the United States. ADS-B information from the deployment indicates it also operated over Abkhazia, which had declared independence from Georgia in 1999 but is viewed by most of the world as being Russian-occupied territory.

In late 2021, the first ARTEMIS returned to the Romanian airport from where it flew sorties to monitor Russia forces near the Ukrainian border. The aircraft flew 370 missions in 2022 – six days a week on average – using its ground moving target indicator to monitor refugee crossing points.

The second ATD is the Airborne Reconnaissance and Electronic Warfare System (ARES), go-ahead for which was given by the US Army in November 2020. On June 12, 2021, the US Army Project Director for Sensors – Aerial Intelligence (PD SAI) awarded a Phase 1 contract to demonstrate, develop, build, and integrate prototype ELINT and COMINT sensors onto an enhanced HADES platform. L3 Communications Integrated Systems and Raytheon Applied Signal Technology received the contract for ARES via the Consortium for Command, Control, and Communications in Cyberspace (C5) which, according to its website, was created to "accelerate the development and deployment of new capabilities to the warfighter through the use of other transaction authority."

Bombardier Global 6500 N799JR (c/n 60032) completed its first flight after

modification as the ARES ATD from Waco in Texas on August 27, 2021. Like the ARTEMIS aircraft, ARES is a contractor-owned/contractor-operated asset and has been deployed overseas. It was in South Korea during May 2022 and at Kadena in July 2023.

The third ATD programme is the Army Theatre Level High-Altitude Expeditionary Next Airborne (ATHENA). It is split into two components, known as ATHENA-R (radar) and ATHENA-S (SIGINT). L3Harris Technologies (as it became in June 2019) and MAG Aerospace were awarded a contract in March 2023 for ATHENA-R, under which they will modify and operate two Global 6500s for the US Army under COCO conditions. The first ATHENA-R airframe, Global 6500 c/n 60107, was registered as N291SR to L3Harris Technologies on August 6, 2023.

ATHENA-S will be based on the SNC Rapcon-X. The Nevada-based company will produce and operate two of the aircraft, again based on the Global 6500 airframe, under the terms of a contract awarded on September 28, 2023. SNC started the 'rapidly configurable' Rapcon-X programme using its own funds in 2021, purchasing two of the business jets (N650RX c/n 60083 and N650SN c/n 60089) which had already been worked on at its facility at Hagerstown, Maryland, prior to the US Army contract. They will be equipped with the Leonardo Osprey 50 active electronically scanned array radar in a 'canoe' under the fuselage and have a satellite communication system along the top of the cabin and are expected to fly within a year of the contract award. Together, the seven ATD jets mark a return to the use of COCO arrangements for the US Army.

BELOW • Artist's impression of the SNC Rapcon-X based on the Bombardier Global 6500, of which two have been ordered as the ATHENA-S, one of four different business jet configurations as demonstrators for the HADES project.
SIERRA NEVADA CORPORATION